PRAISE

WHAT CLIENTS LOVE

"Loaded with great ideas. Buy a dozen copies and give them to your friends and clients. They'll love you for it."

> —Al Ries, coauthor of *The 22 Immutable Laws of Marketing* and *Positioning*

"Don't lend this book to a friend . . . You're unlikely to get it back."

> —Seth Godin, author of *Tribes* and *Purple Cow*

"A provocative take on topics such as branding and customer service . . . Written in short sections, the book is ideal for even the busiest business owner to dip into at any free moment. Read one section a day as a daily 'marketing inspiration.' The only problem: WHAT CLIENTS LOVE is so interesting, you won't be able to put it down."

> —*Entrepreneur*

"Harry Beckwith provides great insight into what customers experience and expect, together with a prescription as to what to do about it. In today's tough competitive environment, managers must understand the power of the customer pull."

> —James Champy, author of *X-Engineering the Corporation* and *Reengineering the Corporation*

more . . .

"Harry Beckwith has written a brilliant book, taking client servicing to yet another level. Read it. If you don't get at least a dozen ideas to improve your marketing strategies, client relationships, and bottom line, you probably should change careers."
—Deena Katz, author of *Deena Katz's Tools and Templates for Your Practice*

"Breaks down our high-tech, ultra-efficient Brave New World of sales, marketing, and advertising into very human terms . . . The author's talent lies in explaining a number of obvious, though sometimes counter-intuitive, notices about what internal and external clients need from marketers. Not 'want' but 'need,' though that's just the beginning."
—*Miami Herald*

"Harry Beckwith's checklist on questions to ask in building an exceptional business is worth the price alone."
—Jack Trout, author of *Big Brands, Big Trouble*

"Harry's advice truly has built our business, and you can get it for a fraction of his hourly fee by reading this terrific book."
—Dick Kovacevich, former CEO, Wells Fargo Corporations

WHAT CLIENTS LOVE

A Field Guide to Growing Your Business

HARRY BECKWITH

BUSINESS PLUS

NEW YORK   BOSTON

This publication is designed to provide competent and reliable information regarding the subject matter covered. However, it is sold with the understanding that the author and publisher are not engaged in rendering legal, financial, or other professional advice. Laws and practices often vary from state to state and if legal or other expert assistance is required, the services of a professional should be sought. The author and publisher specifically disclaim any liability that is incurred from the use or application of the contents of this book.

Business Plus
Hachette Book Group
237 Park Avenue
New York, NY 10017

www.HachetteBookGroup.com

Printed in the United States of America

Originally published in hardcover by Hachette Book Group.

First Trade Edition: June 2010
10 9 8 7 6 5 4 3 2 1

Business Plus is an imprint of Grand Central Publishing.
The Business Plus name and logo are trademarks of Hachette Book Group, Inc.

The Library of Congress has cataloged the hardcover edition as follows:

Beckwith, Harry
    What clients love : a field guide to growing your business /
Harry Beckwith.
        p. cm.
    Includes bibliographical references and index.
    ISBN 978-0-446-52755-2
    1. Marketing. 2. Advertising. 3. Brand name products. 4. Customer relations. 5. Success in business. I. Title.
HF5415 .B4235 2003
658.8'02—dc21

                                                        2002069122

ISBN 978-0--446-55602-6 (pbk.)

Book design by Giorgetta Bell McRee

To you
Dad,
for proving
you were possible.

Contents

Introduction:
A Lesson from the Road   xv

DRAWING YOUR BLUEPRINTS

Your Possible Business   3
A Question That May Be Your Answer   4
Another Good Question   5
Why Plan?   5
The White Hot Center: Nike's Genius   6
Finding the White Hot Center   12
The Fourteen Principles of Planning   13
  1. Forget the Future   14
  2. Stop—Yes, *Stop*—Listening   15
  3. Celebrate Foolishness   17
  4. Resist Authority   17
  5. View Experts Skeptically   18
  6. Beware of "Science"   19
  7. Mistrust Experience   20
  8. Mistrust Confidence   21
  9. Avoid Perfection   22
 10. Beware of Common Sense   23
 11. Embrace Impatience   24
 12. Find the Water   25
 13. Finding the Water: A Warning   26
 14. Search for 100-X   27
The End of "Missions"   28

How George Didn't Do It 30
Fortune Favors the Bold 32
Laurel Cutler's and Ian Schrager's Insight 33
Ask Questions Like a Priest 34
The Classics of Business 35
What Osborn Drugs and Target Tell You 38
New Economy, Same People 41

FOUR BUILDING BLOCKS: ENORMOUS ORANGES AND
CANARY YELLOW BUGS: CLEAR COMMUNICATIONS

Key Trend: Option and Information Overload 45

Your Prospects: Everybody's Talkin' at Them 50
The Rise of Images 51
Your Marketing's Placebo Effects 52
Snap Judgments Stick 53
The Humanist and the Statistician 54
The Clever French Orange 56
Lessons from Stanford's Stadiums 58
What Your Prospects Know 59
An Important Word on Word of Mouth 60
Your Shortcut to Incredible Luck 63
Getting Publicity: The Giant Hole 65
Publishing: Another Surprise Benefit 65
Four Rules for Getting Yourself Ink 66
Testimonials: A Startling Discovery 67
Quoting No One 70
What *Is* an Expert? 70
The Doctor from the Boondocks:
  How to Seem Expert 74
Your Key to Clarity 77

How to Look Expert   78
How to Sound Expert   79
Mark Twain's Marketing Lesson   79
The Boy Who Cried *Best*   81
Why Superlatives Fail Colossally   82
The Dale Carnegie Corollaries: The Power
  of You   83
Rudolf Flesch and the Canary Bug   85
Harpers, McPaper, and Tiger   86
A Lesson from Jefferson's Tomb   88
Shorter Sells   90
How to Read a Sentence   91
Your Final Step: The Frenchman-on-the-
  Street Test   92
Absolute Brilliance   93

THE VELVET SLEDGEHAMMER: A COMPELLING MESSAGE

Key Trend: The Decline of Trust   99

Cole's Wisdom   103
The Faster Way to Be Believed   104
A Wolverine and the Comfort Principle   105
What the Best Salespeople Sell   106
What Ordinary Salespeople Sell   107
How to Read a Short List   107
How to Read a Short List, Two   110
Wield a Velvet Sledgehammer   111
A Game of Give and Take   113
Why Hard Selling Has Gotten Harder   114
What Would Aesop and Jesus Do?   115
Lessons from Colorado: Find the Force   117

What Your Prospect's Nods Mean 118
Why Cold Calls Leave People Cold 119
Sell Like You Date 120
Why Goldman Sachs Cannot Cold Call 120
Remember Eddie Haskell 121
A Trick to Improve Your Presentations 122
L.A. Confidential and The Rule of Contact 123
Lincoln Had No Slides at Gettysburg 124
How to Boost Your Chances 126
Impressive Slide Shows Aren't 127
Remember: It's a *Visual* Aid 127
Packaging the Bold or Conservative Idea 128
Do Like the Romans 129
Keep Talking Happy Talk 130
Dion and the Rule of Three 131
Think Pterodactyls and Typhoons 133

BLUE MARTINIS AND OMAHA SURFING:
A REASSURING BRAND

Key Trend: The Rise of Invisibles
and Intangibles 137

Georges Always Beat Als 140
What's in a Name? 142
The Familiarity Principle 142
To Know You Is to Love You 144
What Fidelity and Vanguard Show You 145
Familiarity and the New 80/20 Rule 146
Understanding Your Brand: Gerber Unbaby
    Food and Salty Lemonade 147
The Limits of Every Brand 150

A Thousand Words?   151
Understanding Symbols   153
Understanding Symbols: The 1965 Pirates   154
Lessons from Lowe's   155
Move Your Message Up   157
Kinko's Cleverness   158
Why Copy Shops Struggle   160
Sir Isaac Newton, Human Being   161
Omaha Surfing and Jefferson Airplane   162
Clients Love Odd Things   164
Blue Martini, Loudcloud, and Other Odd Ducks 165
How to Think Odd   166
Hit Your Prospects in the Nose, Too   168
A Powerful Tool for Branding   169
Finding Your Perfect Name:
    The Descriptive Name   170
The Perfect Name, Option Two: An Acronym   171
Option Three: The Neologism   171
Option Four: The Geographic Name   172
Option Five: The Personal Name   173
Primrose and Yahoo! The Evocative Name   175
A Checklist for Avoiding the
    Lake Tahoe Name   176
Harley, Ogilvy, and the Incredible
    Shrinking Names   179
Churchill Was Right: Your Package Is
    Your Service   180
Imagineering's Six Commandments   182
Clients Understand with Their Eyes   183
Boiled Critter at Tiffany's   184
What Your Space Says to Your Client   187
No Room at the Bottom   188
Laid-Back Heart Surgeons and Other Horrors   190

But It Helps Recruitment 190
Some Help from Hong Kong 191
Just Junk It 192

AMERICANS THE BEAUTIFUL AND *PRETTY WOMAN*:
CARING SERVICE

Key Trend: The Wish to Connect 195

New Communities 196
Starbucks' Key Insight 198
What Your Clients Actually Buy 201
A Lesson from Hong Kong 203
An Insight from *The Great Gatsby* 205
Americans the Beautiful: Understanding
   Positive Illusions 207
Watching *Pretty Woman* 209
Uncertainty and the Importance Principle 211
People Need People 212
Money Can't Buy You Loyalty 213
Efficient Tools Aren't 214
"Thank You, (Enter Client Name Here)" 216
The End of the Line 216
Kohl's Race to Clients' Hearts 218
How Priceline Almost Snapped 220
The Good Neighbors Drop By 221
The Mercer, the Morgan, and the Grand:
   The Power of Welcome 222
Your Fastest Way to Improve Client Satisfaction 224
Four Rules for Choosing Clients 225
The Gift That Isn't 225
Your Clients Were Always Right 226
Keeping a Client's Confidence 227

A Promise Written Is a Promise Kept   227
Your Three Key Moments: 3, 24, 5   229
Understanding Listening   230
Your Silence Is Golden   232
How to Listen   233
A Lesson from the Eastern Oregon Desert:
    How to Remember Names   234
The Rule of "Whole Plus One"   235
Ten Rules of Business Manners   237
Staff Like Spago   238
Ritz-Carlton's Shortcut to Satisfied Clients   239
How Judy Rankin Shot a 63   241

THE TRAITS CLIENTS LOVE

Humility and Generosity   245
Sacrifice   247
Openness   249
Integrity and What It Actually Means   250
What Clients Love Most   252

YOUR GREATEST ASSET

Why do Some People and Businesses Thrive   257

APPENDIX

Checklist: Questions to Ask in Building an
    Exceptional Business   261
A Reading List for Growing a Business   267
An Interview with Harry Beckwith   274

MY FAVORITE PART: ACKNOWLEDGMENTS   279

Introduction: A Lesson from the Road

This book offers a pleasant alternative to learning from your mistakes:

Learn from mine.

My mistakes began with *Selling the Invisible*. Because clients love experts and no one looks more expert than an author, many people called me after the book appeared, often with invitations to speak to their companies. Naturally, I accepted.

I went. I spoke. I bombed.

I flew to Miami to address a leading telecommunications firm. I covered the subjects the employees had loved in the book, but the number of people checking their watches seemed a bad sign. I stumbled on until the clock mercifully signaled the end.

My host grabbed my arm as I staggered from the podium and promised a postmortem in a few minutes. I waited for him in the hotel lobby as the audience members filed by me as if I were hosting a virus. Minutes later my client appeared, sat down at the lobby table, and began the background for this book.

"Good material, really. But let me give you a tip.

"You mispronounced our president's name. *Three times*. That threw everyone off."

I had made the president and his company sound as if they did not matter to me. The employees felt slighted, and because of that, they did not like me— and my speech.

Off to Chicago to talk to some food distributors. Again I covered the content they had loved in the book—*and* correctly pronounced their key people's names. They responded better, but dozens of decibels short of a big ovation.

I knew why as I sat back down. I had viewed the audience as my enemy. I resented their power to judge me; they were blockading my romp to happiness.

Because I resented them, many of them felt uncomfortable; something seemed off—and because of that, my speech did, too. *Clients feel about a service the way they feel about the provider.*

Next stop, Tucson, I was determined to like that audience. I even carried a Post-it to the podium that read: Engage, Help, Smile.

This seemed to work. Everyone listened, laughed, and teared up at the sentimental moments. My slump had ended.

No, it hadn't.

After hearing many compliments as I left the meeting room, I walked through the hotel lobby and down a corridor to the gift shop. I had just started to study a stuffed javelina when a man with a sticker that read "Bend, Oregon," beelined toward me with what I assumed would be a compliment.

"Right up to the end you were a 10. You had us in your palms," he said. "Then you mentioned being divorced. After that, it was a 1. Ruined everything."

Who was this person who could be sidetracked by something so irrelevant?

A typical client.

In this new world, technical skills matter; they pay

the entry fees. But many clients can afford that fee, and most clients cannot distinguish one firm's skill from another's. Competence gets firms into a game that relationships win.

My first book discussed the importance of relationships briefly. My fingers may have been racing on the keyboard, but my heart was in neutral. I still believed that competence wins and superior competence wins constantly.

My mistake.

This book is the lessons from those and other mistakes and the successes of many companies, huge and small. It explores the loves of clients, shaped and altered by four significant social changes. Every business that understands and harnesses these changes, which introduce each of the next four sections, should thrive.

After those four sections, this book explores how to design a better business. The Appendix includes questions that readers can use during that phase.

The book concludes by discussing the most valuable traits of people in this Evolved Economy. Clients love these traits; they have forever.

I have loved exploring these ideas and hope you find insight, inspiration, and many tools here that will help you grow—and enjoy doing it.

Harry Beckwith
October 1, 2002

DRAWING YOUR
BLUEPRINTS

Your Possible Business

Forget benchmarking. It only reveals what others do, which rarely is enough to satisfy, much less delight, today's clients.

Forget studying critical success factors, although the Japanese built an apparent economic dynasty by focusing on them. That dynasty was merely apparent because their foundation question was flawed. The question, "What has made companies in our industry successful?" leads you to the old answers—which leads you to copy and refine rather than innovate.

(The Japanese "dynasty's" preferred copy-and-refinement method was to improve product quality and build at lower cost—two huge American weaknesses at that time. This resulted in $700 VCRs that could be profitably sold for $400, and gave the Japanese a huge but temporary advantage. Because the Japanese approach was a simple refinement of the "critical success factors" in the electronics industries, however, American companies were able to copy the Japanese formula quickly, by tightening quality control and outsourcing their labor to lower-wage countries.)

Never mind what clients say they want. No client ever asked for ATMs, negotiable certificates of deposit, heated car seats, Asia de Cuba, traveler's checks, Disneyland, Cirque du Soleil, or Siegfried and Roy, and no one outside a few thousand techies asked for home computers. Clients never said they wanted any of these things.

Their creators simply created them, sensing that people would love them.

The extraordinary successes—Federal Express, *Lion King* the play, and Citicorp as three enormous examples, and Powell's Bookstores, Creative Kidstuff, and Ian Schrager's hotels as relatively small ones— never benchmarked, studied critical success factors, or polled prospects on what they might want. Instead, each of these companies asked the same question:

"What would people love?"

Ask that question, too.

Ask—and keep asking yourself—"What would people love?"

A Question That May Be Your Answer

Next time you ponder your strategy, ask:

If I ran a competing firm, how would I beat ours?

Which weakness would I attack? What would I do to distinguish this new firm and seize business from our current one?

Then do this: Eliminate that weakness. It is your soft underbelly—the reason you are losing some business.

Then build that distinguishing strength—before someone else starts doing it.

Always ask, "How would I beat us?"

Another Good Question

Whenever you consider your business's next steps, ask, "If we were starting this business from scratch, what would we do differently?"

Then do that.

Now and then, start from scratch.

Why Plan?

Most people assume that business plans will tell them what to do. Few businesses, however, follow their plans. Things change, assumptions change—and plans change with them, as they should. Yet businesses still plan.

Why?

Because the value of planning is not in the plan but in the planning. Planning teaches you and your colleagues about your business, market, customers, and each other.

Like writing a book, writing a plan educates you in a way that nothing else can.

So keep planning. As you implement your plan, your prospects and clients will react, and their reactions will teach you more. Among other things, their reactions, carefully observed, will reveal what clients want—and love.

Plans teach.

The White Hot Center: Nike's Genius

Nike's success—from its awkward beginnings in Bill Bowerman's kitchen near Eugene, Oregon, to its four-hundred-pound-gorilla status today, can be traced to its source: the White Hot Center.

Nike began when Phil Knight no longer felt content with distributing America's then dominant road running shoe, the minimalist, Japanese-made Tiger. He and Oregon track coach Bill Bowerman collaborated to make a new shoe, which they named quickly after the Greek goddess of victory.

In choosing to partner with Bowerman, Knight went straight to the White Hot Center of American running. Bowerman and Villanova University's Jumbo Elliot were American running's gurus and living legends and the coaches of many American Olympians, particularly distance runners. With Bowerman came the other man at the White Hot Center of America's running industry: Steve Prefontaine, America's fastest and most charismatic runner in the events from two miles to five thousand meters, a figure so large that Hollywood would later make not one movie, but two, about his life.

With Bowerman designing the shoes and "Pre" wearing them, Nike quickly became the most visible symbol and name in American running in the early 1970s.

Then Nike struck gold in an unexpected place: Germany.

Frank Shorter's unprecedented and widely watched triumph in the 1972 Olympic marathon in Munich—in what otherwise had been a humiliating Olympics for Americans and a tragic Olympics for everyone—turned America, almost overnight, into a nation of runners. Jim McKay's almost elegiac coverage of Shorter's run—McKay's poetic repetitions of the words, "You must run the race by yourself" may have been the most powerful slogan for running ever uttered—prompted Americans who had not run since PE class to jog a mile the next morning. Fortunately for Nike, these new converts needed shoes.

Nike was launched and continued rising almost vertically through the running boom that followed. But all good things must end, and by mid-1980, the boom did, too.

In fact, the boom was never quite what it appeared. By the late 1970s, owners of running stores shared a secret: Most running shoe purchasers never ran. They simply wanted to look fit and feel comfortable.

Running shoes had become a fashion business.

As both running as sport and running shoes as fashion declined, Americans discovered a healthy and less jarring alternative to running: aerobics. Reebok, a British shoe manufacturer, saw this wave and caught a ride first. Soon women and many men were sporting Reeboks, and Knight's shoe, which stood for victory and had achieved one so quickly, suddenly seemed near defeat.

At this point Nike could not have survived an overt attempt to cast away its athletic image and move to fashion, to be like Reebok. The classic 1980s images of women in slouchy white socks and color-coordinated tights and leotards would work for Reebok. Nike, however, stood for putting in your mileage, not striking a pose. Nike could not be both.

Luckily, Nike didn't have to do anything. An iconic blonde did it for them.

The blonde was Farrah Fawcett, the famously tressed star of the hit TV show *Charlie's Angels,* and her accidental act of philanthropy for Nike was to pose for a photograph. While a poster of a come-hither Farrah in a tight red swimsuit—the Poster-That-Decorated-a-Million-Men's-Dorm-Rooms—became more famous, this photograph of Farrah on a skateboard appealed more to girls. Farrah appeared to be having fun—instead of lusting after their boyfriends.

And she was wearing red and white Nike Cortez shoes.

Few could pull off the famous Farrah hairdo, but everyone could buy a pair of white and red Nikes—and almost everyone did.

Without disavowing its mission of creating seri-

Wolfgang Puck also rose to stardom through a well-executed White Hot Center strategy in creating Spago. After cheffing at the fabled Hollywood restaurant Ma Maison, he opened Spago in Hollywood in 1982, and cultivated the region's most powerful dining crowd: film directors, producers, and stars. Spago's hostesses studied Variety *and other magazines so they would recognize prominent industry people when they entered Spago. Once in, the staff memorized and indulged the star's preferences, however unusual—Suzanne Pleshette's preference for overcooked pasta, for example—an item that did not appear on Spago's menu.*

ous shoes for serious athletes—by merely standing on the sidelines while Farrah worked her magic—Nike got to the White Hot Center: the woman who most influenced mainstream tastes.

Once again, all good fads must come to an end. *Charlie's Angels* went off the air and Farrah settled into marriage. At the same time, people learned that performing aerobics was harder than running. You cannot "do aerobics" anytime, anywhere; you need music, an instructor, and a gym, which may be miles away. Aerobics also proved to be an indoor activity, which made it less attractive whenever the sun shone.

Nike needed a new White Hot Center, and once again found one, not through luck this time, but from the foresight to see a star rising.

By the late 1980s, basketball had emerged in America. Spurred by the star quality of players like Magic Johnson and captivating teams in America's two media capitals and largest cities—Los Angeles and New York—basketball was beginning to displace baseball and football as America's most popular sport.

For Nike, this was bad news and good news. People still saw Nike as a running shoe company; first impressions stick. Nike needed to overcome this limited image. It needed to get to basketball's White Hot Center.

Fortunately, Nike looked ahead.

If Nike had focused short term, it might have tried to enlist Johnson or Boston's Larry Bird to promote Nike basketball. Instead, Nike chose a recent University of North Carolina graduate and—in what seemed odd at the time—a player who was not the first chosen in that year's pro draft of college players.

(Hakeem Olajuwon was chosen first. Nike's neighbors, the Portland Trailblazers, used the second pick to choose Kentucky center Sam Bowie, whose name never appeared on a pair of shoes or an All-Star team roster.)

Nike's choice, as many readers all over the world know, was Michael Jordan. Jordan rapidly became basketball's White Hot Center: uniquely talented, charismatic, attractive, and among the greatest competitors in any sport ever.

Behind the obvious scenes, however, Nike was meticulously working the Centers. It hired men who were close friends with the leading players on New York City's legendary playgrounds, the breeding grounds for Julius Erving, Kareem Abdul-Jabbar, Albert and Bernard King and—in the eyes of New York City kids—even bigger earlier legends like Earl Manigault and Helicopter Heinz.

In football, Nike moved to intercept athletes early in their careers by establishing summer Nike camps for aspiring college players. Nike-hired coaches would hone these players' skills while measuring their performance in the forty-yard dash, bench press, squats, and other metrics that college coaches use to compare prospective players.

In less visible sports, Nike got its shoes into the hands of top players at comically young ages: nine-year-old tennis players and ten-year-old golfers, for example.

Because key media figures also occupy the White Hot Center of most industries, Nike cultivated the media. When it hit an obstacle—as it did in its early feud with the dominant running publication, *Runners'*

World—Nike executives simply called an end run. It bought the rights to the name of a tiny distance running publication with the definitive, White-Hot-Center-of-the-sport name—*Running*—and began publishing its own running magazine.

Nike is one of thousands of American companies that demonstrate the inordinate power of a few influences—the White Hot Center—over an entire industry.

Almost every industry has a WHC. Among architects, for example, the WHC is occupied by the editors of well-respected regional architectural publications; a few writers, notably the *New York Times*'s Paul Goldberger; and several discerning clients—New York's Guggenheim Museum, for example—who are looked to for their views on the best or hottest architects. The influence of this handful of people at a White Hot Center is, like Michael Jordan's in the basketball industry, seismic—a point well made in Malcolm Gladwell's *Tipping Point*.

While Running *died young, the publish-your-own strategy can work. The most spectacular example is the popular financial magazine* Worth. *Fidelity Investments started the magazine when its cozy relationship with* Money *magazine cooled. (*Money *writers and editors touted Fidelity so often that other mutual fund companies, all of them potential* Money *advertisers, complained.) The company that used publishing most nakedly as a promotional device to promote its brand is* Yahoo! *To ensure maximum exposure on magazine stands,* Yahoo! *calls its Internet magazine* Yahoo! *The promotional benefits of this name exposure alone made it worthwhile to publish this magazine at a loss.*

Overwhelmed by options and information, pros-

Many students of the architecture industry and devotees of great architecture increasingly lament the influence of its White Hot Center, bemoaning a trend that critic Ada Louise Huxtable dubbed "trophy buildings by signature architects." Frank Gehry seems to build everything, while other innovative architects have failed to penetrate the WHC and, through it, the attention of prospects. As a result, these exceptional architects work in relative obscurity and rarely make the short lists for potentially significant and conspicuous projects, such as major museum designs or renovations.

pects increasingly look to the White Hot Center before they choose. The Center's seal of approval comforts clients; it assures them they are making a good choice.

Be like Nike. Identify and cultivate the White Hot Center.

Finding the White Hot Center

Who are the experts in your industry?

Which editors, writers, and publications wield the most influence?

Which clients shape the opinions of other clients and prospects?

Which newspapers and magazines do readers respect most? Who publishes, edits, and freelances for them? What is your relationship with these people? Do you have other entrées—friends, colleagues, allies—who can help you reach these key influences?

Where do these members of your White Hot Center meet? What trade shows and conventions?

Develop a map to your White Hot Center and a strategy for cultivating it. Anticipate the next members of the White Hot Center and get to them early—as Nike got to Jordan and Tiger Woods. (Nike CEO Phil Knight followed Tiger for every match in the 1994 U.S. Amateur, even before Tiger declared his intention to turn professional. It is widely assumed that Nike first contacted Tiger no later than Tiger's freshman year—*in high school*.)

Every industry—from national shoe manufacturers to local beauty salons—has a White Hot Center. (What salon does the hair for the news anchors in Portsmouth, New Hampshire, or Jackson, Mississippi? Which clothing store provides their suits?)

Like the hair salon industry in Portsmouth, your industry has a White Hot Center. These questions will help you find and cultivate yours.

Ask these questions to find your White Hot Center.

The Fourteen Principles of Planning

*A*uthor's note:

In the five years since *Selling the Invisible* first appeared, many people responsible for planning in their companies have expressed thanks for the section titled "The Fallacies of Planning." Planning perplexes, plagues, and stalls many managers, not because "our data is flawed." Our data rarely fails us; our ways of thinking do.

To help you implement this book's advice, the following section updates and revises substantially "The Fallacies of Planning." The previous version helped many people; this revision should help more.

1. Forget the Future

The experts said the telephone would promote peace, obliterate Southern accents, and revolutionize surgery.

H. G. Wells predicted phones would eliminate urban traffic congestion, because people would no longer need to work in cities.

The phone's inventor was even further off. He envisioned it merely as a device to transmit musical concerts.

When it became obvious that phones would allow people to talk across distances, most prophets still goofed. Phone company executives envisioned a specific use for the phone conversations: business calls. What about the possibility of people calling their friends just to talk? Preposterous, they thought. Waste of time. Won't happen.

No matter how hard we stare, we cannot see ahead.

Your planning should not rest on suppositions about the future because no supposition—other than death and taxes—is safe. Rest your assumptions instead on the one prediction that has never missed: People will pay for what they love. Plan to build what they love, and let the rest of the future take care of itself—as it always has.

Plan around what you can predict: what people love.

2. Stop—Yes, *Stop*— Listening

For years books have encouraged you to create innovations by listening to your customers.

Stop.

Every day American businesses introduce changes based on what clients said. Conservatively, 85 percent of these changes have no effect. Others backfire completely.

This pervasive plea to "listen more" rests on a flawed assumption: It assumes that people say what they think. They do not. People often say whatever will make them look good to the person asking the question—market researchers for example. Almost no one confesses to drinking too much or fudging expense reports. Thousands of men who teared up watching *The Remains of the Day* insist it was a silly chick film. Few Twinkies fans own up.

The second flaw in the plea "listen more" is the assumption that people understand themselves well enough to reveal themselves accurately. When we search our souls, we know this isn't right, and that Carrie on *Sex and the City* was right, when in show two, season three, she mused:

"Isn't it strange how we can know our friends perfectly, and still not understand the first thing about ourselves?"

We confound ourselves. Young and old go off to "find themselves," searches that rarely turn up much. Like Carrie, Nietzsche was right:

Of all life's mysteries, we are most mysterious to ourselves.

Listen to prospects and clients by all means—but always with mounds of salt.

Psychologists for decades have recognized that words are misleading, and that it's better to observe. "Life happens at the level of events, not words," the noted psychologist Alfred Adler once said.

Trust only movement.

Do not listen; watch. To cut through all the protective layers and get into people's hiding places, look harder and more carefully. Become the very definition of a great researcher; learn to look at what everyone else looks at—and see something different.

Stop listening and start looking.

3. Celebrate Foolishness

A translucent, grape-colored computer that you use at home? For what?

Stranding a dozen people on a made-up desert island to see who survives strenuous backstabbing and infighting—millions will watch that on television? Dumb.

A $3.75 cup of coffee? Get serious.

People love the new and different—if only because it makes them feel they are progressing, renewing themselves, growing. Only by escaping what others have done and doing what no one has done before can you become new—and achieve huge break-throughs.

Think dumb.

4. Resist Authority

Assemble eight people in a room and what happens? The Alphas take over.

As a result, the ideas that are implemented in your company do not come from the good thinking. They come from the Alphas—the animals in any cluster that seize and hold the power.

Are Alphas good at creative or strategic thinking? Not necessarily. They are just good at seizing power.

Often, they are only the people who *look* the most powerful—as studies show that the taller a business school graduate, the higher his or her starting salary.

If you are an Alpha, learn to keep still and wait.

Listening to authority will focus you on the past, on what has worked. But little is working today; discontent with services is at record heights. Listen to authority and you will repeat this shadowy past—and lose your clients.

Question authority. (Quietly.)

5. View Experts Skeptically

As that rarest of jokes—a one-liner about economists—goes, expert economists have correctly forecast thirteen of the nation's last six recessions.

Meteorologists assure you there is little chance of rain at the moment you are looking out the window, noticing a cloudburst.

The movie experts at Universal Studios said no to *Star Wars*.

What qualifies someone as an expert? Lots of data and experience. But to what end? We regularly find two experts on opposite sides of almost every question, each armed with data to support their arguments.

The expert George Soros, one of the world's wealthiest men and most famous investors, was so certain that global capitalism would fall that he wrote a book on the subject. Just two years after the book appeared, Soros looked around, saw that capitalism was flourishing, and confessed to the *New York Times*.

"I goofed," the expert said.

Beware of expert advice. Too often, the expert is applying previous experiences to a current one. But any time we apply the lessons of one experience to another, we assume those two experiences are identical.

They never are.

Question experts.

6. Beware of "Science"

People frequently say, "The research shows."

Research outside the hard sciences—and much of the research *in* them—never shows anything. Research merely suggests; it suggests a tenable conclusion.

We overvalue research, particularly when its conclusions are expressed in quantified form. "Most people like twenty-four-hour Internet access" sounds weak to us. "Five of six people like twenty-four-hour access" sounds more accurate and reliable; "83.3 percent of all respondents like twenty-four-hour access" sounds like a scientific fact worthy of immediate action, even though that statement is identical to the statement before it, and drawn from the same research used to support each of these conclusions.

Research assured Ford that Edsels would sell like

Hershey bars, prompted Columbia Pictures to pass on *E.T.,* and encouraged Richard Zanuck that the movie *Star!* would be a huge box office success.

"We're home," he wrote his father, Daryl, after hearing the results from *Star!* 's first previews.

"Better than *Sound of Music!* "

Mistrust research. It rarely reveals what clients really love.

7. Mistrust Experience

For years, Dr. Stephen Jay Gould carried fond memories of sitting with his father on the steps of the famous tennis center in Forest Hills, just outside Manhattan in Queens. Several years ago, Gould was walking in his old neighborhood and noticed those steps.

They led to the dilapidated door of Mueller Moving and Storage.

We remember things that never happened. We cite as proof for something an event that did not happen as we remember it.

In Daniel Schacter's *The Seven Sins of Memory,* the author alerts us to how poorly we perceive events, citing recent cases where DNA evidence showed that 90 percent of eyewitness identifications of the perpetrators of crime were wrong. Yet "they saw it with their very own eyes"—something we regard as convincing proof.

We read about a fever over tulips in the Netherlands that led some Dutch people to pay a fortune for a single bulb. We draw a parallel to our stock market, and conclude that stocks have become like tulips.

Then we find *Famous First Bubbles* by Peter Garber, and learn that tulip mania probably wasn't what we've believed for years. No economic slowdown—much less a downtown—occurred when the Dutch tulips crashed. Yes, they fetched ludicrous prices—but they do today, too. An anonymous buyer recently paid $700,000 for a single bulb. There has always been tulip mania, orchid fever, and similar passions.

Our experiences, like our impressions of tulip speculation, eyewitness observations, and memories of Forest Hills, often were not experiences after all. They are fictions we have read or written ourselves, but that we treat as fact.

Mistrust your experience and your memory.

8. Mistrust Confidence

We are wrong more often than we know—especially when we are sure we are right.

It happens so often that social scientists have given the syndrome a name—the Overconfidence Bias—and have demonstrated its extent in several studies. These studies asked people a series of questions, then asked them to indicate their confidence in each answer, from a minimal percentage to 100 percent, or total confidence.

What happened?

Fifteen percent of the answers in which they were totally confident were wrong. *Whenever you are certain of something, you are wrong 15 percent of the time.*

This has at least three implications for planners. First, try to locate that 15 percent in your business—those areas in which you are consistently acting on mistaken assumptions or conclusions—and attack those mistakes.

Second, question yourself constantly. Even when you are certain you often are wrong.

And finally, don't allow other people's strong convictions to sway you, or adopt the point of view of the most confident advocate. Many people merely use confidence as a tool of persuasion, and appear certain because they want to prevail. Still others are sincere in their convictions—sincere, but dead wrong.

If you feel certain or someone else does, question it.

9. Avoid Perfection

Getting to "best" always gets complicated.

First, can everyone agree on what is best?

How long will they take to reach that agreement?

Once they agree, how long will it take to execute that "best" tactic? Can it really be executed efficiently, swiftly, and well?

Plans in business usually obey the Rule of Start-Ups: Everything costs twice as much and takes twice as long as expected. Can you afford that much time and money?

"I am not seeking perfection. It's unattainable. What I am striving for is professional excellence."
—*Tiger Woods*

How much excellence must you sacrifice in other areas—work environment, productivity, speed of delivery—to achieve excellence in a particular one?

And will prospects and clients perceive that excellence? Will it benefit them? Will they care? Will it be worth to them what you charge?

Shoot like Tiger: for excellence, not perfection.

Good beats perfect.

10. Beware of Common Sense

A Fortune 500 executive once suggested that marketing is relatively simple. It's just common sense.

Common sense, however, is neither common nor always sensical. Albert Einstein once dismissed the entire notion, calling common sense "the collection of prejudices we acquire by age eighteen." The historian Barbara Tuchman devoted an entire book to this subject. In *The March of Folly,* she chronicled five legendary acts of foolishness, including Montezuma surrendering to a Spanish army no larger than a fifth-grade class, and the Trojans hauling that wooden horse into their city.

Common sense can protect you from colossal mistakes. What it cannot do is inspire enormous breakthroughs. Common sense inspired none of the great marketing innovations of our lifetime—not traveler's checks, negotiable certificates of deposit, overnight package delivery, or the Absolut vodka campaign.

Leaps of imagination created them.

Common sense goes only so far. Breakthroughs require imagination.

11. Embrace Impatience

Most organizations seem to believe in inertia. They believe that things tend to stay as they are, either at rest or in motion, and therefore that progress begets progress, inevitably.

The rule of exercise applies instead. Moving organizations tend to keep moving. Ones that rest—on their laurels or otherwise—actually atrophy, grow weaker, and die young.

To worsen the problem, not moving never looks like a bad idea at first, because nothing immediately goes wrong and signals the dangers of standing still. Hey, we waited to make sure we were right and nothing bad happened, so that's good.

As a result, not moving inspires more not moving.

Employees become dormant, too, no longer faced with new challenges and new positions. A few employees tolerate the condition; the creatures of habit and opponents of change actually relish it. But dynamic people require dynamic environments. Go dormant and those action-oriented employees will bolt, taking your greatest source of vitality with them. Without these people, your organization becomes even more waiting-oriented. You grind to a halt, then shift into reverse.

Exercise works with businesses, too.

12. Find the Water

The planning group assembles, discusses their options, and reduces them to one. Let's assume for illustration the option was Plan A of 1999: Implement Our Internet Strategy.

Essentially, this company has decided that to quench its thirst and need for growth, Plan A will provide the water. The company sends everyone in that direction.

The problem is that nothing in marketing is guaranteed; you never know where the water is until you find it. Too often, the water proves to be the Mirage and the company finds itself high and dry, having spent money and time; it has depleted its water supply to find a new supply.

Now, with less water than when it began, the company's survival is threatened.

What should you do instead? Spend less time planning and more efforts on inexpensive dispatches of small parties to several likely locations. When those scouts return, assess what they learned and which pond represents the best source. Then focus all that time and money you saved on *that* expedition.

Dip your toes in several ponds, then dive into the lake.

13. Finding the Water: A Warning

Like many events in business, this one sounds comically familiar. We do not know if any water is out there, the executive reports. Let's wait until we are certain.

This is like waiting for the water to come to you. Not since Noah has this happened.

The company that waits for guarantees is doomed. Nothing in business is guaranteed. Past successes are simply past successes, not guarantees of future ones.

Do something—if only because doing produces learning, and learning is perhaps a service business's most valuable asset.

Do.

14. Search for 100-X

Venture capitalists (aka VCs) are well known for their abbreviations for mega-returns on investment. What the famous investor and author Peter Lynch calls "ten-baggers" (an investment that appreciates tenfold), VCs called "10-X."

Looking for greater returns to compensate for their many high-risk investments that fail, VCs look for investments that could appreciate 100 times, or 100-X.

In fact, a typical venture capital portfolio shows that the 80/20 Rule—that 80 percent of all good results come from 20 percent of your activities—understates the difference between good business ideas and the great ones. One or two of a VC firm's investments produce enormous returns; the rest produce virtually no returns, or near-total losses. A 90/10 principle actually applies.

The 90/10 principle applies to even the tiniest storefront business: All strategies are not created equal. Terrific strategies and tactics more than beat good ones; they work hundreds of times better.

Move your thinking, time, and money into one or two possible 100-X strategies. Quickly test different strategies and tactics, then spend every penny you can find—and borrow—on the 100-X strategy.

Every minute and dollar you spend will repay you back many times, while pursuing the other strategies will just divert you from success.

Look, and keep looking, for 100-X.

The End of "Missions"

Blame the Blues Brothers.

Today, people associate "missions" with catastrophes (the *Challenger* mission), and crackpots (Reverend Jim Jones's mission to Guyana). John Belushi and Dan Aykroyd skewered missions in *The Blues Brothers*. Asked to explain their havoc-wreaking behavior, the Brothers claimed, "We are on a mission from GOD."

The word "mission" has lost its force. Comedians spoof it while others use the word to suggest overzealousness or anger ("Jeez, the boss was really on a mission today!"). Most executives and employees now view "missions" as the product of another year-long, Corporate Initiative Du Jour that generates nothing but takeout pizza orders and a document that is taken no more seriously than the regular requests to please keep the coffee room clean.

In the final blow, Dilbert mocked mission statements by offering Catbert's Mission Statement Generator (formerly hosted at http://www.dilbert.com/comics/dilbert/career/bin/ms2.cgi), which created all-too-familiar missions such as "our mission is to continue to assertively customize cost effective content as well as to continuously revolutionize market-driven intellectual capital."

So state your mission—just don't call it a mission statement. Call your mission what it is: your purpose. It is your reason for coming to work, your passion, your deeper reasons that go beyond bringing in and divvying up the money.

Ask, Why are we here? What is our passion?
What do *we* love?

At ServiceMaster company, people work to do God's work. Mail Boxes Etc. employees work to make people smile. Before its sale to French Telecom in the summer of 2000, Orange employees worked to help people live easier and better lives. Millions of Americans work for the love of doing a common thing uncommonly well.

Whatever your purpose is, stating it *works*. The statement of purpose for ACI Telecentrics hangs conspicuously behind its receptionist's desk, where it impresses so many visitors that many ask for copies. A powerful statement of purpose attracts and comforts clients, inspires employees, and produces measurable results.

> *A signal that it is time to change a name or phrase is when it is ridiculed in a popular movie, and provokes a big laugh. On this point, health maintenance organizations should review the movie* As Good As It Gets—*and rethink the name "HMO." Few scenes in any movie provoked louder laughter than Helen Hunt's rant:*
>
> *"H...M...%@#@#%ing... Os!"*

Define your purpose. Call it "Our Bigger Purpose," or "Why We Are Here," or "The Difference We Will Make." Whatever you call it, remember the Blues Brothers—and don't call it "Our Mission."

Define—and rename—your mission.

How George Didn't Do It

Perhaps George H. W. Bush struck the fatal blow. Asked to assess his sputtering 1982 presidential campaign, he confessed a weakness:

"Oh, the vision thing."

The word "vision" was near death anyway. Being pragmatic by necessity and usually by nature, most executives struggled with the idea of creating their vision—partly because of the word itself.

Vision, as defined in the Random House Dictionary of the English Language, Unabridged:

"An experience, generally regarded as beneficent or meaningful, in which a personage, thing, or event appears vividly or credibly to the mind, although not actually present, under the influence of a divine or otherwise spiritual agency or under the influence of a psychological or physiological condition. Cf. hallucination."

We didn't make this up.

We equate visions with imaginings, pipe dreams, and hallucinations, with Ebeneezer Scrooge in *A Christmas Carol* and his visions of the Christmas ghosts. Scrooge's ghosts were unreal, of course, as visions always are.

Business, however, abhors the unreal, partly because the real challenges are big enough. Visions sound impractical, ethereal, unreal. You must change that by changing the word.

You must rename your *vision.*

A different name will make it clearer to others what a vision is and does. To find that new term, let's define these two controversial words, "mission" and "vision."

A mission is your higher purpose: It is the broader societal impact you want to have. Merck's mission is to improve human health; Disney's, to provide joy; Lettuce Entertain You, to offer people an enjoyable escape; Greene Espel's, to provide a community for gifted lawyers and clients.

Visions, by contrast, are selfish. *Visions are your long-term aspirations for your business,* not for those that you might serve: to be the best-regarded, most profitable, or most reliable, for example. Visions involve no higher purpose and no mission to help mankind, although achieving your vision can have that added effect.

To illustrate, John F. Kennedy once clearly expressed one of his visions, or goals for the group that he led, the United States of America: to put a man on the moon. He knew that goal was enormous and that the thrill of reaching it would inspire and invigorate almost every American. That was his vision: America will put a man on the moon.

Behind Kennedy's bold vision of accomplishment was a mission—a greater purpose: It was to create a world without war and its threat. Certain that America's intentions always would be peaceful, he believed that the moon could give our country a military advantage so great that other nations would negotiate peace rather than consider war.

A man on the moon was Kennedy's vision; world peace was his mission.

Call your vision what a good vision is. Call it "Our Business Goals." If you want a more inspiring term, try "Our Target" or "What We Will Be." If you prefer something more concrete, try "Our Firm in 2005." Choose something practical and businesslike.

Then identify that concrete goal—and aim high. A modest goal will inspire modest effort, make the ride less exciting, and dilute the thrill of reaching your goal. If Kennedy had articulated the relatively modest visions of "A woman on Everest" or "A 38 percent improvement in the balance of trade," it wouldn't have inspired Americans at all, or elevated our country's stature in the world.

Bold yet achievable concrete goals—like "a man on the moon"—will inspire your people's passions, particularly if you package them to emphasize that they are bold goals rather than corporate clichés.

Create and communicate your vision, but rename it.

Fortune Favors the Bold

When an admirer praised him for *Walden,* Henry David Thoreau insisted that a greater achievement was within every person's reach. "To affect the quality of the day," Thoreau said, "that is the highest of arts."

The author of another famous work—a bumper sticker—offered a variation of Thoreau's comment: Perform random acts of kindness.

Each man offered a starting point for defining the purpose of your enterprise: What can you do to make people's lives better? That people would love? That could matter when you are gone?

The answer to those questions—answers that might affect the quality of people's days—is your purpose, and while those answers may sound bold and grandiose, that is precisely the point: It is the bold and big statements that inspire people, attract clients, and give people's lives meaning, long after the money's been counted.

In crafting your statement of purpose, aim very high.

Laura Cutler's and Ian Schrager's Insight

"Nice is nowhere," the noted marketer Laura Cutler once said. "You do not want everyone to like what you do.

"You want 10 percent to love it."

"Contentiousness," the skilled marketer observed. "That's the key in a good name. People love the feisty and unexpected."

Ian Schrager created and runs a revolutionary chain of hotels, including New York's Paramount and Royalton hotels. His properties are to hotels what Salvador Dali paintings are to art—not for everyone. Schrager expressly designs his hotels for one traveler in twenty-five. "Let twenty-four despise them for all I care," he has said.

"Just so one in twenty-five love them."

Can any marketer afford to be that provocative? Can you write off 96 percent of the public?

Apparently. Schrager's hotels *net* more than $20 million a year.

If everyone feels comfortable with your idea, it isn't an idea. It's an imitation. Push beyond that toward the edge, toward something like a fingerprint—something so distinctive it resonates powerfully with a few.

Avoid "nice."

Ask Questions Like a Priest

A man feels guilty about a sin and goes to his Catholic church. He opens the door of what looks like a wooden closet and sits down. Concealed behind a screen in the closet, so the parishioner cannot see him, is the priest. The man begins to confess his sin.

Why does the church choose this unusual ritual?

Because it knows something: The ritual encourages people to speak honestly. The screen protects their anonymity. Remove that anonymity and the person becomes less open and honest.

Put someone into a focus group, for example, and who does she become? Someone who others will like, respect, or fear—whatever her goal.

She becomes someone else.

Sit a person in front of an interviewer and you get a similar result. Rather than speak honestly, she tries to make an impression—just as thousands of voters did in 1980. Wanting to sound generous, those voters told interviewers they would vote for Carter. Then they went into the hiding of their voting booths and voted for Reagan.

Make sure your subjects cannot see their interviewer. (And make sure they know that their names will be kept secret.) Like concealed priests, anonymous interviewers get more truthful answers.

Many people yell or slam down the phone at telemarketers. They are willing to look ugly because their caller cannot see them. Similarly, customers interviewed by phone speak far more critically than customers interviewed in person. The customer on the phone is not afraid to appear impatient, angry, self-important, and even neurotic.

To get to the truth, use phone interviews by independent third parties. Like the priest behind the screen, those third parties will get candid answers and you will get more accurate insights into your customers and prospects.

To get the truth, get on the phone.

The Classics of Business

Some key answers to your marketing questions are not where you may think. They are in the hearts and minds of clients, who are human: rational and irrational, hopeful and fearful, elated and deflated. Because they are human, the question "What do clients love?" can be asked better:

What do *people* love?

This better question points us in a better direction. It directs us past the Business section, where we find books about "clients," and eventually to Literature, where we find classics about people.

Who in history, after all, best understood human character? Most experts agree on the answer.

It was Shakespeare. Authors of books of quotations devote more pages to Shakespeare's words than those of any other author, for a good reason: He had more to say. His now legendary characters such as Hamlet, Othello, Iago, and Falstaff lived hundreds of years ago, yet you can find them all over the world today. They are classic types, and they help us better understand people of their types and others—if for no other reason than that there is a little Hamlet and Iago in all of us, a little melancholy one moment, avenging and clever the next.

We call Shakespeare's plays "timeless" because his insights are; his observations about people are as pertinent now as they were in Elizabethan England.

To illustrate the value of fiction in uncovering the insights that you need, imagine that you are targeting "ambitious, upwardly mobile suburban women employed in sales."

Begin from the beginning: What does "ambitious" mean, and how do you tap into that trait? You can read market research on "strivers" forever and never equal the insights on American ambition in Theodore

Dreiser's *Sister Carrie* and F. Scott Fitzgerald's *The Great Gatsby,* decades old yet still deadly accurate.

What does it mean that your prospect is "suburban"?

You could rely on crude stereotypes—or read the deftest descriptions of American suburban life yet written: John Updike's Rabbit Angstrom series and John Cheever's dark *Bullet Park.* You also could study ten reputable profiles of salespeople, including the typical salesperson's Myers-Briggs profile, and learn far more from three scenes of Arthur Miller's *Death of a Salesman.*

Your prospect teaches college instead? Read *Moo* by Jane Smiley or *Crossing to Safety* by Wallace Stegner. (*Who's Afraid of Virginia Woolf?* reveals a side of that life, too.)

Works in high tech? Douglas Coupland *Microserfs.*

Lives in Manhattan? Tama Janowitz's *Slaves of New York.*

African-American? *Waiting to Exhale* by Terry McMillan.

These authors, good and great, spent years asking the question at the heart of the humanities: What does it mean to be human? Their answers help you find yours, the key question at the heart of this book:

What *does* a client love?

In 1996 I asked eighteen top executives and business advisers to name the best business books ever written. Surprisingly, only three books got more than one mention. *In Search of Excellence* and *My Life with General Motors* each appeared twice, as did the third and most startling title on their lists. This epic sprawled over 1,100 pages and had morphed into a miniseries in which no character transacted any business, at least as Westerners define it.

The book was *Shōgun,* James Clavell's novel of Japan.

The two men who named *Shōgun* knew that one key to growing a business was understanding people, and that fiction is filled with facts on that subject.

Novels reveal what clients love.

To understand Business, check Literature.

What Osborn Drugs and Target Tell You

Osborn Drugs in Miami, Oklahoma, pioneered the commercial use of the Internet. In 1996 it created an easy-to-use Web site, publicized it well, and waited for the cash to roll in.

It didn't roll. It crawled.

The site produced modest growth—about 5 percent annually. More significant, however, was where that added 5 percent came from: 90 percent of the people using the site already were customers.

The Web site, in the end, has not changed Osborn Drugs's business. It has merely tweaked it, shifting a few store buyers over into online buyers.

Osborn Drugs learned that for most businesses, the Internet is not an enormous marketing tool. It just creates one more communications medium and distribution channel that can attract a few new customers and help you satisfy your current ones.

For nine businesses in ten, the Internet is a customer service tool.

Target stores seem ideally suited to Internet marketing. They offer good commodity products, from Jolly Ranchers to patio tables, at excellent prices. Target also has managed its brand so well that it has made discount shopping cool and made its low-cost products stand for quality—a feat.

> *"This is my biggest frustration: All the clients who are convinced of this pent-up demand for their services that will just explode the day they get their Web site running."*
>
> —IT consultant, Dallas

So Target is one company that should thrive on the Internet. Yet listen to what its CEO predicted for the Internet, years into Target's Internet effort. "The Internet will emerge," Robert Ulrich said, "as a good shopping channel in certain categories."

Note those words. Not a *great* channel in all categories or a good channel in *most* categories, the Internet is merely a "good" channel in "certain" categories.

Ulrich added that the Internet offered limited potential for sales volume and profit—an understandable view, given that Ulrich's average Target stores currently outsell Target's entire Internet operation.

Obviously, there is a killer Internet application for one particular business: Web sites that allow buyers to comparison shop for commodity products—virtually

The Internet does provide a valuable channel for one service industry: college alumni organizations. The Internet enables online chats, messages, searches for old college chums, and online seminars, to name a few uses. The Internet also helps eliminate an obstacle to the success of these clubs: distance. At least 90 percent of the typical alumni association's members live too far from campus to participate in campus activities.

identical products sold primarily on price. A Web site that allows a contractor to comparison shop for construction materials ranging from nails and concrete to lumber and glass, for example—now if any Web-based business can succeed, that's the one.

Yet this business has been tried, executed well, and failed.

The reason reveals volumes: "Low prices are not enough," many contractors said after these sites failed. "We want good products, on time, from people we trust."

Year 2001 Beckwith Partners	
Estimated new business inquiries	*Total*
From all sources:	*325*
From firm Web site:	*3*

The Internet is not your business. It merely supports the fundamentals of business—basics that the Internet does not change.

The Internet is merely an aid and never the answer.

New Economy, Same People

The psychologist Judith Badwick described our world perfectly: "The economy is new," she said.

"But the people are old."

We still love things that we can see and feel. We prefer the touchable to the intangible. Golfers, for example, have learned that you cannot "virtually" play Pebble Beach golf course. Like pregnancy, you either experience it or you don't. You must experience Pebble Beach itself; nothing comes close.

The virtual never satisfies our appetite for the real; it only whets it.

We love the real and resist the fake. We detest, for example, ads in which two actors who presumably never wash their own clothes rave over a new detergent. We cringed when Mr. Robinson advised the Graduate, Benjamin Braddock, that the future was in one word: "Plastics."

We laughed in Mr. Robinson's face: plastic: phony, unnatural, unreal—everything we disdained.

Meanwhile, information technologies barely affect millions of services, from cutting lawns to cutting hair. In these businesses, the Internet functions like a telephone—a simple tool of communication—and as an electronic brochure. The Internet has changed one type of business: anything involving the sales of intangible commodities, such as stocks and auto insurance. The Internet reduces the time and costs of the salesperson-middleman, and allows certain businesses, such as discount brokerages and booksellers, to thrive.

> *"Strategic inflection points—truly revolutionary and disruptive technologies—are exceedingly rare."*
> —*Michael Porter, Harvard Business School*

But beyond those services, the Internet has transformed little.

Consider marketing consulting, which seems well suited to an Internet transformation. The Internet enables a client to choose, hire, engage, and work with these consultants without ever seeing them. Yet marketing consultants fly more now than ever, and meet their clients face-to-face more frequently, not less.

People in these firms have learned that electronic contact, rather than enhancing client-consultant relationships, can damage them. Context communicates volumes—but e-mails lack context. Nuance and emphasis are missing; a direct message can sound cold; your gentle joke can be missed because the recipient cannot see your tongue in your cheek.

The electronic message seems impersonal.

Soon, the relationship feels impersonal, too.

The Internet gives but takes. By lulling us into thinking that electronic communication can replace face-to-face contact, the Internet leads us to neglect our relationships—which we cannot.

You must become more personal, not less.

FOUR BUILDING BLOCKS

---

1. Enormous Oranges and Canary Yellow Bugs: Clear Communications

KEY TREND: OPTION AND INFORMATION OVERLOAD

It is the best of times, it is the worst of times.

Dickens described eighteenth-century London with those opening words in *A Tale of Two Cities,* and more than two hundred years later they seem to apply to our lives. Our plight, however, is different. Unlike Dickens characters, Americans do not suffer from having too little. We suffer from having too much.

Freud suggested this in *Civilization and Its Discontents.* Living in our age of relative abundance, Freud noticed something missing: happiness. We became more civilized and less content.

Not surprising, really. We tried to leap from caves and fires to split-levels and Cuisinarts, and to live through revolutions while we progress by evolution, little changed from our ancestors of two thousand years ago.

We crawl; life races past.

Our abundance overwhelms us. In 1970, we could buy a regular or Princess phone, in black or avocado, in wall or counter model. Those were our options.

Today, our choices seem infinite; no one understands all of them. Call waiting, call forwarding, caller ID, intercom? Wireless web? Sprint, ATT, Qualcomm? Fifty hours? Five hundred? Is 100 @ $29.95 better than 200 @ $39.95? Should I get DSL? Wait: What *is* DSL?

Look longingly at the 1970s again. A typical middle-class American had a checking and savings account, life insurance, and maybe some bonds, stocks, and land.

Contrast that with today: Stocks and bonds, 401 (k)s and their rollovers, inherited IRAs, deferred and defined benefits programs, charitable trusts, Clifford trusts, dozens of other trusts, annuities (variable and otherwise), nonqualified deferred compensation, thousands of mutual funds—oh, and including loads and no-loads, indexed and nonindexed, value, growth, and blended, small-, mid- and large-cap. Options become suboptions, multiplying like mice, overwhelming even the experts. An executive at an annuity company, for example, recently confessed to me that he cannot stay current on annuities. How can the rest of us, then, understand annuities *and* our several thousand other options?

We can't. So we don't bother to try.

NUMBER OF U.S. MUTUAL FUNDS:

1984: 1,241
1999: 7,791

Consider something as old and seemingly simple as music—and consider the poor music buyer and the retailer. This year record companies will release more than 21,000 titles—almost sixty a day. Who can keep up? No one. Can a great band without a brand label and an expensive public relations blitz get its name in front of *Rolling Stone,* the retailers, the radio stations, and, most important, the buyer who might love their CD? Barely, rarely.

Overload.

Prospects have changed because of Option Overload. Knowing they cannot know and understand all their options, they increasingly choose the most trustworthy and seemingly competent person—or choose no one at all.

"You seem like a good and honest person who knows what she's talking about," today's client decides. "You're hired." Today's clients cannot choose among services and products—they cannot gather all the information.

So they choose among people.

Technological option paralysis: The phenomenon, named by Douglas Coupland in his well-known book Generation X, in which a prospect for a computer or product finds so many options that he feels paralyzed and does not buy at all.

Researchers at Stanford University recently found that we suffer option paralysis with even simple products. Faced with a few varieties of jams and jellies to choose from, most people will buy at least one jar. When given more options, however, they usually leave empty-handed.

Just as we are overloaded with options, we are awash in information. The *New York Times* recently estimated we are exposed to 3,200 commercial messages every day. We see ads on the sands of beaches and in the borders of TV programs. Soon we will turn on the TV news and see a Russian robot on the moon. On its side we will notice two words:

Radio Shack.

Or perhaps we won't see those words. A massive Microsoft logo might be obscuring them. (A British ad agency plans to make this possible by using lasers to project ads onto the moon.)

Back on earth, the city of Atlanta recently considered selling its street names to corporations. Imagine the corner of Bell South and Coca-Cola, where the grocery features a floor with a T Rex–sized image of actress Jasmine Bleeth wearing a Got Milk? mustache.

Messages, messages everywhere. In 1970 there were 334 morning newspapers in America; today there are 736. The average cable television viewer in 1996 chose from forty-seven channels; today it's fifty-five. Fifty years ago we heard that television would kill radio, yet the United States adds new radio stations at a rate of almost one every day and more than eleven thousand in all.

Messages, messages everywhere. In 1472 a person reading a book a month could finish every book in the world's best university library (Queens College in Cambridge, England) in less than twenty years; the college's mammoth collection comprised 199 books. Today, American companies publish almost three hundred books *every day*.

Messages, messages everywhere. They besiege us in airplanes waiting for takeoff and at basketball games waiting to tip-off. Their siege forces us to listen selectively and, as the din grows, to stop listening completely.

Consider your parallel experience. If you meet someone at a party you will try to remember her name. If you meet six people at once, you will nod as the sound waves hit your ear, but you know better than to try to retain their names. Overload.

Your prospects are reaching a similar saturation point. Which means that unless you can break through this noise and into the prospect's heart, you will be whispering in a hurricane.

No one will hear.

No one wants to listen; the torrent of words has overwhelmed us all. As Nobel-winning economist Herbert Simon has said, a wealth of information creates a poverty of attention. The more there is to hear, the less we listen.

The more information proliferates, the more the contradictions and, with them, our confusion grows. Information tells us that Acme tires are perfectly safe and that Acme tires are dangerously defective; that tech stocks are a bonanza and a death wish; that Tom Cruise is seeing another woman and that Tom Cruise is seeing another man. We have more information but more confusion, more data but less confidence.

We are drowning in information and screaming for knowledge.

The apparent experts—those with insight, wisdom, and knowledge—will prosper, as they help us filter through the noise—or simply assure us we need not listen. We can simply listen to them.

This complexity and noise influences prospects in another way. In life as in physics, actions inspire equal and opposite reactions. Growing complexity makes us covet the simple. Consider the revealing history of the book *Simple Abundance* and its sequels. Fifteen years ago, Sarah Ban Breathnach pitched the idea for these books to dozens of publishers, each of whom rejected her. Who cared about simplicity then? No one.

Who cares about simplicity now? Almost everyone,

it appears: Her books have sold more than six million copies.

The present belongs to those who can sort through this abundance of choices and information—the simplifiers, the filters, the clarifiers.

Let's see how you might join them.

Your Prospects: Everybody's Talkin' at Them

We are in the world of *Midnight Cowboy*. In that film of the same name, Jon Voight plays an unsophisticated Texan in New York. As he walks New York's streets a song captures the feeling of being a simple person in an increasingly complicated world.

He hears the words "Everybody's talkin' at me." What happens when everyone talks at you? The next words of the song answer that:

"I don't hear a word they're saying."

No one can hear when everyone is talking. So when everyone talks, no one can hear, so everyone stops listening. This has several implications.

First, don't talk when everyone else is. Advertise where your competitors do not, so that your message differs from what people are hearing.

Second, say little. A single point penetrates. A mass of messages merge into a blunt object that penetrates nothing.

Third, speak visually. We often cannot hear words, but we notice images, especially appealing ones.

Fourth, make each word count. If people learn that your communications rarely say anything, they will stop listening, even when you *do* have something to say.

To be heard you must say something different, simple, and visual.

The Rise of Images

Because so many words have lost their value, the business looking to grow should turn to two weapons: actions and images.

Actions have always spoken louder than words, and now that words and claims have become more suspect, that gap has widened.

Your actions are your message.

So ask: How must we act to convey our message and quality? What must we *do,* from our first follow-up call to presentation? Then, imagine that you must sell the client without words. What images would you use?

How would you dress when you meet them?

Never mind words—how do you act and look?

Your Marketing's Placebo Effects

You think a pill will make you feel better and so, it does. It's the famous placebo effect.

This effect goes beyond medicine, and right through your door every day.

You enter a lobby and think, This must be a good firm. And so it is. You meet a prospective manager for your investments and decide she seems smart. And so she is.

You are surrounded by placebo effects, constantly working their alchemy. We have the experiences we expect to have, based on our perceptions that preceded those experiences. Our perceptions create our expectations—and those expectations so influence our experience that we can say this:

Our expectation changes our experience.

Social scientists call this Expectancy Theory. People experience what they expect to experience and see what they expect to see. Our challenge in marketing, especially invisibles, is to shape these expectations. We need to manage placebo effects.

Do you create the expectation that you will be skilled, reliable, trustworthy? Does your business card? The people who answer your phones?

Does your advertising distinguish you? Do you look better, smarter, more successful? Does your lobby beat your competitor's? What does your briefcase say? Are your materials made with better materials?

Is your Web site smart, quick, and clear?

In this world of placebo effects, how are yours?

Study everything that can affect people's perceptions of your quality—and make each excellent.

Watch and manage your placebo effects.

Snap Judgments Stick

You see a two-second clip of a prospective service provider. You then are asked to evaluate him using a fifteen-point checklist.

What if you saw a five- or ten-second clip instead? Would more information lead you to a different evaluation?

Now, what if after you completed those assessments, you worked with Will for three months? Would your assessment be different than your snap, several-second judgments? You answer, "Of course." Those added months would lead you to a more informed and accurate assessment.

No, they would not. Your well-informed assessment will resemble your snap, two-second judgment.

Harvard psychologist Nalini Ambady discovered this when she asked college students to assess a professor after viewing a two-second video clip of the professor in action. Later, she asked them to evaluate the professor from five-second and then ten-second tapes. The students' assessments did not change.

Dr. Ambady then waited for the end of the semester, when she asked the students to fill out the fifteen-point evaluation. The entire semester had little effect. The students' opinions at the end of the semester were very similar to their assessments after the first two-, five- and ten-second exposures.

This suggests we are wrong to say that first impressions merely last. First impressions are *eternal*. As Malcolm Gladwell observed from Ambady's research, first impressions become self-fulfilling prophecies. We make immediate judgments about people and then we fit everything we see to conform to our snap judgment.

The first seconds are make-or-break. Rehearse them, and ask others to help you prepare for them: the right dress, the right materials, the right watch, the right key message. The first seconds shape every second—and month—that follows.

Master the first seconds.

The Humanist and the Statistician

People's first impressions are plagued by stereotypes that you must control.

Mr. Gladwell found a dramatic example of stereo-

typing in Ambady's research. She gave the students
one added piece of information. For group one, she
identified the teacher as a professor of statistics. For
group two, she identified him as a professor of humanistic psychology. Same teacher, same clip, different title.

The students' assessments changed, too. The statistics professor was "cold, rigid, remote, picky, tense."
When the same man was labeled a "humanistic psychologist," however, what happened?

Students said he was "warm, deeply concerned
with helping students, great man."

*Yet he was the same man—the "cold, rigid, remote"
man.* Which leads to a critical rule of marketing:

People's stereotypes—about you and your industry—become their lasting opinions.

Consider the plight of financial planners. For
decades they have been burdened with their label.
People dislike planning—both the idea and the word.
Planning sounds tedious and difficult. It also sounds
like it will produce steps that people must follow, taking away their freedom. At the same time, the word
"financial" reminds prospects of a private, sensitive
subject: their money. People barely understand their
money and how it might work better—and you ask
them to plan something around that?

The words "financial planning" frightened prospects
away.

A former trial attorney turned creative director-
copywriter once learned about the sheer weight of
stereotypes when he presented a proposed ad campaign to a computer monitor manufacturer. The manufacturer's director of marketing loved the campaign.

He raved several times during the agency presentation and several times, two days later, when he called the agency president to announce he had chosen another agency instead.

The ex-attorney's boss responded to this news predictably. "But I thought you loved the campaign!" he said. "What was wrong?"

"Nothing. It was very creative—the best I saw. Great!"

"Then why'd you choose the other agency?"

"Because I just don't think a lawyer can be creative."

Watch your labels and descriptions and ask yourself what they might communicate about your company. Ask if they play into stereotypes or negative reactions, and look at alternative labels that create better impressions—or more favorable stereotypes.

Study your description carefully and consider changing it.

The Clever French Orange

After reading about digital video recorders for ten months, Leon Joseph decided it was time to buy.

He walked into the VCR section of his favorite electronics retailer in TriBeCa in New York City. No digital video recorders. Where were they? In the music section: Leon's first clue.

He found the two best-known devices and asked

the clerk to explain the differences. The clerk couldn't; the clerk had no idea how either machine worked. In an odd role reversal, Leon ended up explaining the products to the salesperson.

A case study in poor service? Perhaps. The DVRs had been on the shelves almost a year—enough time for every clerk to learn about them.

Leon's experience, however, offers another example of complexity—and the need for businesses to address it.

For inspiration, Leon's favorite store and every other business should consider the huge success of Orange, the wisely named international telecom company. Its executives' personal experiences with phone services, reinforced by their interviews with phone users, convinced them that their industry had a problem. The overwhelming array of pricing plans was confusing prospects.

Orange responded. It eliminated every plan but one.

Then Orange kept simplifying. It gave every client just one number and person to contact for service, for example.

These innovations helped Orange retain the customers attracted by its powerful brand message, "The future is bright. The future is Orange." Its customers loved Orange's simplicity so much, in fact, that the company's client retention rate doubled the industry average.

The Oranges of this Evolved Economy will flourish because clarity and simplicity comfort the Leon Josephs of this world, the people overwhelmed by all their options and the information—that is, everyone.

Simplify everything.

Lessons from Stanford's Stadiums

Twenty years ago, this never would have happened.

When Gerhard Casper stepped down as president of Stanford University in the spring of 2000, an experienced university observer might have predicted that his final act would be to initiate a major fund-raising drive or endow several chairs.

Instead, Casper announced that at an estimated annual loss of more than $1.5 million, Stanford was banning all advertising in its basketball and football arenas.

Casper was speaking for millions. He longed for message-free zones.

Americans love their freedom from *everything*. We do not want government butting in. Indeed, we so crave our right to be left alone that our Constitution is the world's only one that scholars have interpreted to create a right of privacy.

Oregonians expressed this desire vividly when they enacted the country's first laws banning billboards. They wanted to behold their state's abundant natural beauty. They wanted for Oregon what they wanted for themselves: to be left alone, unpolluted by demands for money or attention.

Oregon's story tells marketers something about prospects. You cannot intrude in clients' or customers' lives. The more you intrude, the more you annoy.

People love their privacy, crave anonymity, and want to be left alone.

Intrude in people's lives and you risk losing them forever.

Beware where you try to sell.

What Your Prospects Know

Prospects know that Sun Microsystems, Fidelity Investments, and State Farm Insurance are excellent and successful companies.

They know because they keep hearing about these companies on television, reading about them in newspapers, and seeing their ads in magazines and on TV.

What do people know about companies whose names they know only from their mailboxes—companies that send them junk mail? That phrase tells you: They associate those companies with garbage.

As a result, prospects know something that you should, too. They hear *from* bad companies, and hear *about* good ones.

Companies that advertise often and well become familiar to their prospects. Advertising comforts prospects; they assume the company must be at least good. Because of that, advertising warms every marketing and sales effort that follows it.

Warm your direct mail—and all your other marketing efforts. Advertise.

An Important Word on Word of Mouth

"We realize that the best advertising is word of mouth," the CEO announces at the annual meeting at the Ritz-Carlton in Naples, Florida. "Our performance will drive our success—so performance is where we will focus our marketing."

The following year, that company met in a hotel some called "Spartan" in a place that many attendees referred to as "Siberia."

The theory behind word of mouth makes sense: Perform brilliantly and everyone will tell everyone.

But largely because of changes in our culture, word-of-mouth advertising—with notable exceptions, such as book publishing—has become the world's most overrated form of marketing.

Just two generations ago most residents of every American city had lived there for years, often with parents and grandparents nearby. Generations of families knew generations of other families, creating the networks over which word-of-mouth messages raced.

Now look around. Our parents retire and move "someplace warm." The rest of us move to opportunities, one year in the Research Triangle, the next New York or Austin.

Our mobility propels us away from these old networks and into new cities where everyone seems to come from somewhere else.

The relative complexity of our lives reduces the

role of word of mouth, too. Not long ago, when you needed a lawyer, for example, your friend would recommend an attorney in one of your city's two largest firms. Today, competition has forced lawyers, like other professionals, to specialize more—which means that the "lawyer" who would've been appropriate thirty years ago is not the "labor law attorney specializing in Title 7" you need today.

What's more, the people who recommend those Title 7 specialists to others often are not relying on word of mouth at all; they read about the attorney in a local magazine or newspaper.

That is not word of mouth at work; that's public relations—and that is typical.

Jeanine asks Karen to recommend an architect, Karen realizes she hasn't heard about Venturi & Pei for months, which makes her wonder. Afraid to make a bad recommendation, she makes none, or—eager to please and seem informed—she suggests Meier & Gehry or Diller & Scofido. "I've heard great things about them."

Where did she hear about them? In a magazine article about Mr. Meier and Mr. Diller, generated by their public relations people.

Word of mouth assumes your clients will rave if you perform well. But today's clients race home after work, then rush for four more days. When they finally get time to reflect, they have forgotten their good experience with you. They're overloaded.

And who raves these days? Who raves at a party, "You should have seen our tax return—it was brilliant!" Who stops a friend on the street and insists, "You must get your checkup at Methodist—mine was wonderful!"

We rarely rave. We're too jaded and focused on other things. We don't engage in that 1950s leisurely over-the-back-fence chat with our neighbors; those chats disappeared with *Ozzie and Harriet.* If Ozzie were alive today, he'd rarely be home to chat—and if he were home, his neighbor wouldn't be.

These were the networks over which word of mouth flowed—and those lines have gone dead. Progress killed them.

The decline of word of mouth is vivid in an industry once dominated by word of mouth: wealth management. For decades, members of the golf club, the symphony board, or the Junior League typically chose their advisers based on the recommendations from fellow members. Today, however, barely one in three wealth management clients first heard about their firm from a friend, colleague, or relative. Almost half heard about the firm from an advertisement.

These figures are derived from the 2000 VIP Forum survey of affluent Americans. The Forum is a valuable source of insight on financial marketing, particularly to affluent audiences, and we thank them for their generosity in sharing these results with our readers.

Word of mouth has become endangered, and only companies willing to suffer that plight should rely on it or try to promote it—which offends most customers and prospects, by the way.

Forget word of mouth, but do not forget advertising. With the demise of word of mouth, conventional advertising has become even more important.

The best advertising is advertising.

Your Shortcut to Incredible Luck

In 1988 I wrote my first article on marketing and learned a dramatic marketing lesson.

Relying on my experience as an attorney and marketer, I wrote "Is Legal Advertising Different?" for the magazine *Minnesota Law & Politics*.

That October, a Minneapolis law firm associate noticed the article. The byline seized her attention. She knew me. To impress her boss, Cliff Greene, the firm's partner in charge of marketing, she stopped by his office with a photocopy of the article.

"Excellent piece," her Post-it read. "I know the author and think he could help us." Greene read the article and called me—and cracked open the safe. For years his firm used my counsel and convinced other firms to use it, too. Business flourished.

But nothing like it was about to.

In 1994, Greene also was serving on the strategic planning committee at his temple and felt frustrated. Temple Israel planned like most organizations: glacially. "Before this," Greene said, "I thought only the universe was infinite."

Greene asked how I coped with this process. I raced in several directions, mentioned the minefields in planning and how he might avoid them. My response inspired Greene and made him hopeful—especially if I would talk to his group. I agreed.

I spent several days writing down ideas for the presentation, then wrote and printed out the speech.

It went well. The committee felt they could complete their plan quickly.

Then another twist, this one accidental.

A week after the presentation, a nationally known art director, Sue Crolick, asked me to critique one of her presentations. Sometimes frugal, I wrote my critique on the back of my draft of the temple speech.

The next morning, Sue knocked and almost flew through my door. What *was* that on the back of my notes? she asked. A speech on planning, I told her.

"Get it published!" she said.

Her plea soon resulted in the article "Why Plans Fail" in *Twin Cities Business Monthly*. Editor Jay Novak loved the article and, later, his readers' many responses to it, and soon invited me to lunch. "Any other article ideas?" he asked. I had one about marketing service businesses and popped out with a title: "Selling the Invisible."

Novak loved the title. "Do it!" he said, without hearing what might actually follow the title. I did. Life changed.

Calls came, letters came, business came. All because one day years before, I'd written an article that a Minneapolis attorney liked.

One little magazine article. One ordinary call.

One stunning result.

Publish. Anything can happen.

Getting Publicity: The Giant Hole

Mark Pincus, the co-founder of Freeloader, was surprised by how much publicity he received—and offered the reason why you will find it surprisingly easy to get your articles published.

"The media is a black hole," he said, "that cannot get enough stuff to suck through it."

The media needs you.

Publishing: Another Surprise Benefit

"Only in writing do you discover what you know."

—Anne Beattie, author

Many universities require their professors to publish as a condition of earning tenure. Why? Because they know something: Nothing teaches like writing.

Among other lessons, writing teaches you that you never write just what you know. You write what you learn as you're writing.

Ideas come to you and trigger other ideas. Thoughts crystallize and connect with others, and the combination of the elements produces a compound: an insight. You learn.

Writing is thinking, and rewriting is rethinking. You ask, "Does this say what I mean to say?" You answer no. You keep going.

You get it right.

You realize you did more than just write more clearly; you have thought more clearly. You've made your ideas better and more useful. In doing that, you have made yourself more valuable—and clear—to your prospects and clients. You've assured them you are an expert—comforting news that every client values.

Writing teaches everyone—especially the writer.

Four Rules for Getting Yourself Ink

Before writing an article for publication, make note:

1. Demonstrate respect for the editor by studying the magazine, determining its goals, and writing a query letter that reveals your study and understanding.

2. Never cry wolf. Pitch weak ideas as strong ones and editors will learn to mistrust you. Instead, you want them to see your envelopes and think, "He always has good ideas worth looking into."

3. You are not selling a story. You are selling happy readers—people who will enjoy your story and think better of the publication because of it.

4. Thanking an editor for running your article makes it sound as if you believe she published your article as a favor; it impugns her integrity. Instead, praise her staff for their valuable help.

Before contacting an editor, review these steps.

Testimonials: A Startling Discovery

Three surprising events occurred in the months before my first book, *Selling the Invisible,* appeared in bookstores.

The first occurred in June 1995, when *Selling the Invisible* appeared as a five-thousand-word article in *Twin Cities Business Monthly,* and almost immediately inspired letters and calls from as far as Atlanta and Scottsdale.

Days later, a literary agent read the article and called, encouraging me to write a book. He later helped me write a proposal in which we included many of those letters that raved about the article. We were certain the letters would stun the publishers into a bidding war.

They didn't. Makes no difference, one said.

Event three, March 5, 1997: The book finally appears. The cover features a shiny red starburst in which is printed a remark from a best-selling business author, who calls the book "a classic." On the back cover are seven other testimonials.

Over the next three years, at least three hundred readers of the book approached me. I asked at least two hundred why he or she bought the book.

The number one reason: liked the format. Among other nice features, the book fit nicely into an airplane carry-on.

Number two: A friend recommended it.

Number three: the title.

Of those two-hundred-plus readers, *not one* reported noticing or remembering any testimonial.

Story two: I tour the country giving speeches, and many attendees send me letters with compliments. At the same time, many other people call to ask me about speaking to their group. I send those callers a packet that includes three pages of these testimonials, including each reference's name and phone number.

These testimonials seem powerless. Dozens of callers thank me for the packet but request a short videotape that shows me speaking. "We really need to *see* you in action."

Three pages of giddy testimonials, and they still wonder, Can I speak?

Yes.

File those two stories and consider this last one. In the August 5, 2000, Minneapolis *Star Tribune*, a reader could learn that there was not one "Best Picture of the Summer." There were seven. The testimonials for the other twenty-six movies seemed to promise that every reader would enjoy those movies. Each movie was wonderful, these testimonials insisted, but our experience told us otherwise.

We have learned to mistrust testimonials.

Testimonials have lost nearly all their original value. New York theater critics can still close a play with one review because they've earned credibility with their readers. But unless your reference enjoys that strong relationship with your prospects, not even the giddiest testimonial will nudge them.

Testimonials *should* work. They once worked. Then people abused, misused, and overused them. The kind words lost their force and readers lost their faith and trust.

By 2001, movie executives faced strong evidence that testimonials were losing their force. In cities like Boston, where critics loved Almost Famous, Cameron Crowe's rock and roll movie/autobiography, people stayed away. In cities where critics panned the movie, attendance was above average. Earlier that year, the movie Wonder Boys followed a similar pattern.

When do testimonials work? When the person testifying has special authority and credibility, or if other evidence is offered that makes the testimonial seem more credible. They also work if they are on film, because the person hearing the testimonial can evaluate the person's sincerity, passion, and credibility.

In every other case, however, people aren't listening.

Beware of testimonials.

Quoting No One

A client sends you a letter of lavish praise, and you immediately see the promotional value. You can quote from the letter to persuade other prospects to become clients, too.

Unfortunately, you cannot use that person's name. His company forbids it, or makes getting clearance to use it so difficult that you cannot endure the delays and red tape.

Should you use the testimonial without listing the author's name, or the name of his company?

No.

Anonymous testimonials set off alarms. The reader notices the missing name more than the words, and wonders why your reference insisted on anonymity.

How do *you* respond, after all, when you see an anonymous quote? You assume the quote is a trick and that no one said it.

So do your prospects.

No anonymous quotes.

What *Is* an Expert?

How do Americans view experts—and what might make them regard you as one?

To understand, it helps to look back.

Our first colonists did not come to America looking for better theater or creative outlets. They came seeking freedom and opportunity. Most of them lacked education, and few stressed learning. Most were Protestants, a group who believed that salvation came through hard work.

These ancestors despised the class distinctions of their native countries and instilled in their succeeding generations an idea that become immortalized: All people are created equal. Americans soon and forever became known as egalitarians, from which it became easy to assume that all people remained equal, developed equally, and deserved to be

> *Max Weber's* The Protestant Ethic and the Spirit of Capitalism *is famous for developing this thesis of the relationship between America's Protestant roots and the development of capitalism.*

treated as absolute equals. A person who refused to do that and thought himself better was "putting on airs"—an expression that conveys the American notion that a sense of superiority, like air, lacks substance or weight.

Perhaps more than any culture, our ancestors focused on the practical. Pragmatism, cost-benefit analysis, and hard work seemed to operate best here. Soon Americans were rich, a happy circumstance that demonstrated the wisdom of being practical and working hard. It was an easy leap for Americans to conclude that common sense and hard work had created their country, while class distinctions, birth, and an emphasis on the arts and scholarship distinguished the distrusted English and the French.

The view that Americans are almost uniquely anti-intellectual is brilliantly developed in Richard Hofstadter's award-winning book, Anti-Intellectualism in American Life.

Americans also began to believe that theories were for fussy people with too much extra time. Teachers and scholars became suspect. Asked to free-associate the word "professor," Americans today still will answer "absentminded," which was a catch phrase—and a Fred MacMurray movie title—by the mid-1960s.

Amercans' mistrust of academic credentials has also been revealed by research on jurors. This research suggests that expert witnesses with degrees from elite schools are viewed no more favorably than experts from other schools. In some cases, people actually view the elite education negatively, even voicing a dislike for the word "elite" itself.

Our antipathy to scholars and scholarship became vivid in the 1952 presidential election. Voters faced a choice: war hero Dwight Eisenhower, who'd graduated near the bottom of his West Point class, or the professorial, Harvard-educated Adlai Stevenson.

The race was over the minute the stereotyping began. People dubbed Stevenson an egghead, a label that stuck, resurfaced constantly, and doomed Stevenson. Americans don't cotton to scholars and thinkers.

Americans mistrust analysis. Often, when you hear the word "academic," a revealing adverb precedes it: "merely." Americans, in fact, regularly use "academic" to describe something that does not matter even if it is correct, as in "Who cares? It's all academic!"

Americans tend to mistrust academic credentials and scholarly writing and presentations. We disdain the person who speaks with too much authority. We cherish humility, even in people we suspect may be brilliant.

Be careful, then, about relying on vitae, credentials, and advanced degrees, even in services that may require them.

Americans invented the term "street smarts," and prize people who combine common sense with a common touch. They also tend to assume that people with an uncommon, scholarly mastery of a subject lack those common but necessary skills—a warning to any firm thinking about touting its individuals' impressive credentials.

Aspiring lawyers for decades have assumed that the only necessary marketing strategy is to attend an Ivy League college and a top ten law school, serve on the Law Review, and clerk for a federal judge or state appellate court judge. While those credentials benefit lawyers specializing in appellate work, the most academic area of legal practice, and affect hiring decisions in many firms, few prospective clients regard these credentials as significant. They believe that anyone able to graduate from law school and pass the bar meets their requirement for intelligence and perseverance.

Find a common way to communicate your uncommon skill.

The Doctor from the Boondocks: How to Seem Expert

What convinces people that you excel?

Your clearest evidence is just that: clearness.

The evidence for this comes from America's courtrooms. Each day, lawyers call experts to testify with the hope that the jurors will trust their expert more than their opponent's.

But which experts do American juries actually "buy"—and, by extension, which of two service firms will appear more expert to a prospect?

One of the world's premier jury consulting firms, DecisionQuest, interviewed thousands of jurors and concluded that Americans do not associate academic credentials, awards, or the expert's conviction and confidence with expertise. Instead, they regard the person's ability to communicate clearly as the strongest evidence of that person's expertise. The clearer the communication, the more expert the communicator.

Clarity is expertise.

> *An increasing number of ads confront the problem that businesses do not communicate clearly. KPMG adopted the theme, It's time for clarity. Dell Computer's ads showed their competitor's salesperson telling a computer customer, "Bear with me while I put this in terms that nobody can understand."*

The legend of the late Harry Beckwith, Jr.—which appears in *The Invisible Touch*—illustrates this point perfectly.

"Dr. B." had never been supervised by a senior surgeon after completing his residency in Maryland, practiced 95 miles from the nearest teaching hospital, and diluted his surgical practice by also serving as a general practitioner with the Rinehart Clinic and Hospital in Wheeler, Oregon.

Dr. B. also diluted his practice with water, in a sense. That water came from the nearby North Fork of the Nehalem River. In those streams he spent every moment he could cultivating his gift for fly-fishing—a talent so special that the government of British Columbia eventually named one of its eastern lakes Lake Beckwith, to recognize the many Kamloops trout Dr. B. coaxed from its waters.

Yet despite all his disadvantages and his relatively routine, tiny-town surgical practice—hysterectomies, tonsillectomies, and appendectomies, which my father himself referred to as plumbing—and yes, those many hours wading the North Fork—Dr. B. would become a legend. By the mid-1960s the people of Tillamook County considered him more than just a good doctor. They began sharing the news that medical experts had named him one of the world's three great surgeons.

It never happened, of course. Few even knew the Rinehart hospital existed. Those who did knew it for its nonsurgical work with rheumatoid arthritis.

So why did the people of Tillamook County view my father as one of the world's leading experts?

Because he communicated *brilliantly*. In language

American business may have discovered the value of clarity. In a National Association of Colleges and Employers survey of 480 companies and public organizations, the quality most sought by employers was not motivation, which ranked third, or academic credentials and performance, which ranked sixth. It was the ability to communicate.

In Grammatical Man: Information, Entropy, Language, and Life, *Jeremy Campbell addresses the relationship between brevity and clarity. He writes, "In nearly all forms of communication more messages are sent than are strictly necessary to convey the information intended by the sender."*

Ironically, he could have cut his sentence in half, and said: "Most people say more than they need to convey their message."

every injured Holstein farmer or log truck driver could understand, Dad could explain a patient's diagnosis, prognosis, alternative treatment courses, the pros and cons of each treatment, his recommendation, and his patient's likely length of rehabilitation and recovery.

Dr. B.'s clarity made him more than *an* expert. It made him *the* expert.

Clarity cuts through the fog and conveys your value to a prospect. Clarity assures the prospect that you will not cloud the issue or confuse the sale.

Clarity moves the prospect from confusion, which aggravates every person's fear of the invisible, to confidence. Clarity breaks down mistrust. Clarity wins.

Prospects often tell service providers "We will get back to you." Sometimes this means they are not in a position to decide—they may be short on funds or consensus, for example. Far too often, however, it means they aren't clear.

Which means their service provider wasn't clear.

To be seen as an expert, be clearer.

Your Key to Clarity

In communicating, your greatest enemy isn't just the noise all around you—it's the noise you create, unwittingly.

What noise do you create? William Zinsser, in *Writing to Learn,* describes it:

"Noise is the typographical error and the poorly designed page. . . . Ambiguity is noise. Redundancy is noise. Misuse of words is noise. Vagueness is noise. Jargon is noise. . . .

"Clutter is noise; all those unnecessary adjectives ('ongoing progress'), all those unnecessary adverbs ('successfully avoided'), all those unnecessary prepositions draped onto verbs ('order up'), all those unnecessary phrases ('in a very real sense'). . . .

"Information is your sacred product, and noise is its pollutant. Guard the message with your life."

Noise discourages readers and pushes them away. It marks you as a maker of noise, a force not to be reckoned with. It can doom your noblest efforts.

Read carefully what you have written, rehearse carefully what you will say. Watch for noise and stifle it. When you do, the message that remains will race to your audience as a pure signal, and they will receive it—and become more receptive.

Send signals, not noise.

How to Look Expert

What do experts do?

Americans perceive as experts the people who regularly speak and write. (Teachers do not enjoy this perception. Americans view teachers as experts on theory—and because of that, as experts only on theory.) "Experts" appear in trade and general publications and address businesses and associations. We assume that people who write and speak must have something valuable to say.

For your firm to be perceived as expert, your employees should publish.

Begin by finding the specialized publications that reach your ideal prospects. Figure out the editor's goals for each publication and the articles they favor. Then brainstorm article ideas that would make the editor who reads your proposal think, "Our readers would enjoy this."

Once your article is accepted, try to dominate that publication. Get articles by your employees published at least four times a year, and run ads for your company in those publications in other months.

Publish. And when you publish, try to dominate that publication.

How to Sound Expert

Before you start writing for publication, remember what first-time author James Simon Kunen observed in his preface to *The Strawberry Statement:*

"Writing is difficult enough without having to make it comprehensible."

Writing is hard work. (As one author famously put it, "Writing is easy. I just sit at my typewriter until blood starts pouring from my forehead.") If you want to appear expert, your writing must be expert: professional and clear. But unless you write for a living, your writing may look foggy. Most people write just a little better than they draw.

Retain a professional writer with magazine-writing experience to help you. It will make you look even more expert to your prospects.

To sound like an expert, hire one.

Mark Twain's Marketing Lesson

A chief executive—that's *the* chief executive, right? Not today.

Cap Gemini, the consulting firm, had nine chief executives before merging with Ernst & Young. Representatives of Bertelsmann are unsure how many U.S.

chief executives they have. A representative told the *New York Times* the company had "eight to ten."

Cap Gemini and Bertelsmann are merely following ad agencies, who pioneered title inflation by bestowing "Vice President" on 40 percent of their employees, a habit that inspired one art director to confide, "We pass out titles like chewing gum."

Economics reminds us, however, that when you produce more units of a commodity, the value of each unit tends to go down.

Words obey this rule.

World-class, leading-edge, ISO900 certified, superior quality, cost-effective, commitment to excellence, proactive—no one believes them anymore. Everyone knows of several companies that proclaimed they were world-class right up to the morning their lawyers first trudged into bankruptcy court.

Overused words do not work. Instead of relying on words at all, offer evidence. Offer the compelling stories—the case studies, awards, business growth, achievements—that make those adjectives unnecessary.

One useful practice: Review every marketing-related communication and try to eliminate every adjective and adverb. Most adjectives and adverbs say nothing, add extra words, and weaken your message. ("Smiled broadly," for example, reads and sounds much better than "beamed.")

> *"Advertising has annihilated the power of the most powerful adjectives."*
>
> —*Paul Valéry*

Eliminating adjectives and adverbs also will discipline you to prove your claims rather than simply make them.

Follow Mark Twain's simple advice. Three simple words on adjectives, he wrote:

Leave them out.

Remove every adjective like "excellent," and replace them with proof.

The Boy Who Cried *Best*

It's clear what the person who first wrote the words "a commitment to excellence" had in mind, but what was the second person thinking?

As Strunk and White famously recognized in *The Elements of Style,* most readers view clichés as a signal to stop reading.

Clichés simply make white noise, and make prospects decide that you have nothing to say, or worse, that you are being deceptive. When they see lazy words—which is what clichés are—they sense a lazy company. Review every communication and strike out every cliché. Among other benefits, your edited copy will appear more interest-

> *And examine this cliché, "a commitment to excellence." If the firm had achieved excellence, it would say that. So "a commitment to excellence" actually implies, "We aren't there yet." Not compelling.*

ing, which will lead more people to read it and respond to it.

No clichés.

Why Superlatives Fail Colossally

Remarkable!

Extraordinary.

World-class.

Superior.

These words do not merely fall on deaf ears; they
deafen the ears of those who hear them. Use these
words and you might as well keep silent.

The Elements of Style once again offers the best ex-
planation why superlatives sabotage your entire message:

> When you overstate, readers will instantly be on
> guard, and everything that has preceded your
> overstatement as well as everything that follows
> will be suspect in their minds because they have
> lost confidence in your judgment or poise. . . . A
> single carefree superlative has the power to de-
> stroy, for readers, the object of your enthusiasm.

A French writer once captured this problem suc-
cinctly, in a warning to every marketer:

"We always weaken whatever we exaggerate."
No superlatives.

The Dale Carnegie Corollaries: The Power of You

"No word sounds as lovely," Dale Carnegie observed, "as our own name." Merely hearing our name makes us feel closer and more important to the person uttering it.

Carnegie's advice can be taken two steps further.

The first corollary applies to your advertising. To illustrate it, look at the following copy, which appeared in the first three advertisements of a February 2001 issue of *Time:*

"That's why Microsoft gives you a complete set of software building blocks."

"Now Fidelity gives you a complete overview of the market."

"With over 10,000 NAPA Autocare Centers nationwide, it's like taking a certified technician with you wherever you go."

See the pattern?

It's the word "you," which rarely appeared in the early years of advertising. For decades, advertising copy reflected the obvious fact that the ad was talking to millions of people: The ads spoke to large groups, referring to the company's customers and prospects in the plural—as "people," "a woman," and "men," for example. So a typical old ad would read, "Mermaid Lotion caresses a woman's skin and restores its natural glow. Mermaid. For the skin women love."

Then someone discovered the Carnegie Corollary. He realized that people reacted more strongly to ads that used the word "you," as if the ad was addressed only to that reader. The new Mermaid ad promised lotion that "caressed *your* skin" and was designed "for the skin *you* love."

The more personal word "you" worked—as Dale Carnegie would have guessed. Because it sounds personal, even intimate, "you" involves the reader personally.

The second Carnegie Corollary applies to presentations. If you begin your presentation and fail to mention your prospect's name in the first minute, the prospect will tune you out. Every time you mention the company by name, each person will shift forward and focus on you. Your reference to them works as a "you"—the most beautiful word in any language.

> *The editors of* USA Today *also understand the Carnegie Corollary. Their stories invite readers in with headlines such as "Tiger Woods: We Love Him." By using the word "we," the headline implies that the reader is part of the story.*

Using "you" also compels you to think about those prospects. You start becoming more client-focused because the word directs your focus toward them.

Use "you."

Rudolf Flesch and the Canary Bug

A popular novelist once wrote, "She walked into the room and served him a bowl of berries and cream."

Change three words, add two, and notice the effect: "She trudged into the musty den and served him a crystal bowl of strawberries and cream."

From his original sentence you learn almost nothing. You can't picture the scene or the woman or sense how "she" feels.

From the revised sentence, however, you learn and sense more. She feels burdened; she trudges rather than walks. She once had money—she has a den and crystal dessert bowls—but her fortunes apparently have changed because the room smells musty; she cannot afford a house cleaner.

The novelist's sentence used fourteen words to convey very little. The revised one, with two more words, says far more. The first sentence is general. The second is specific; specific words such as "crystal bowl" and "strawberries" paint clearer pictures—a key task in selling things people cannot see.

Just as important, the second sentence engages the reader. Specific words do just that, as the researcher Rudolf Flesch discovered decades ago. We are more apt to read a paragraph with a proper noun than with a general one: "Froot Loops" grabs us; "presweetened cereal" does not.

The word "car," for example, does nothing to involve the reader. "Canary yellow VW Bug," on the other hand, paints a picture and may even make you smile. It draws you in. Most people dislike abstractions, but love things they can *see*.

Flesch's research on readability—including insights on ideal sentence and paragraph length and the special power of proper nouns—was adopted by the editors of Reader's Digest *and captured in his 1946 book,* Art of Readable Writing, *which is still in print.*

Similarly, "our colossal growth" says nothing. It sounds dubious, hyperbolic, and immodest. "Over 25 percent annual growth" works better, although the number is so perfectly round that many readers will question its accuracy or credibility. "26 percent annual growth—42 percent above the industry average"—that sounds more credible, informative, and impressive.

Be specific.

Harper's, McPaper, and Tiger

Although *Harper's* magazine attracts literate and educated readers, its best-read section is neither an article nor even a long paragraph.

It's a list: the famous Harper's Index.

No one would call this list graceful, much less literary (a typical item: Amount the U.S. government spent on peaches in 2001: $3.66 million). But *Harper's* sophisticated subscribers read it so avidly that the magazine published a compilation of the lists as a book.

It's not just the teeming masses who crave brevity, the millions who love *USA Today* because reading it requires so little time. Most Americans read like they eat; they graze. They have time for blurbs but rarely enough for stories.

Politicians insist on sound bites because news programs demand them, having learned that viewers tune out longer messages. No verbal meals, please, Americans say.

Give me a bite instead.

We abbreviate everything. We no longer worship the Bobby Joneses, Johnny Unitases, and Broadway Joes. Now it's Tiger, Britney, and Tupac.

Everything is shorter quicker faster—to the point where a separate book could demonstrate that human beings may be in the early stages of developing a new, abbreviated form of communicating—because people want it short quick fast. Especially your prospects.

Get faster fast.

A Lesson from Jefferson's Tomb

Author of the Declaration of American Independence
of the Statute of Virginia for Religious Freedom
and Father of the University of Virginia

Those are the twenty-two words on Thomas Jefferson's gravestone, and all the words needed to suggest his stature.

Why then, do so many companies require several thousand words to convey their qualifications?

Strange but true: Jefferson's gravestone merely lists the three achievements of which he was proudest, and United States Secretary of State and United States President were not among them!

It is because we suffer a handicap. While articles fret about American education under the familiar headline "Why Johnny Cannot Read," we cannot write. We are not taught.

Until now, few have worried about this handicap. Confident of our skills and ourselves, we feel certain that we can write; we've been doing it all our lives, after all.

But everywhere you look you find evidence that we cannot make ourselves clear. "You said meet me at 2:00 A.M.!" "No, I said two o'clock. I assumed you knew I didn't mean two in the *morning!*"

"You said you'd have the report on Tuesday—that's today." "Yes, but I told you that yesterday, which was

Monday. If I meant to communicate that I'd deliver the report today, I would have said tomorrow."

Consider this sentence from a well-known firm's brochure: "[Company X] has migrated from an applications services provider to select EDI-based firms to one of the nation's leaders in offering systemic enterprise-wide solutions and support for inter and intra-office information processing and communications . . ."

The writer of that passage felt confident she was communicating. Before most readers reached the period at the end of her sentence, however, they became ex-readers.

The more you say, the thicker your forest of words. No reader will get lost among three trees. Among three thousand, almost all will.

Cut trees. Count the pages or words (computer word count commands can do this for you instantly) in every piece of your communications.

> *Buy* The Elements of Style *by William Strunk and E. B. White. This gem of a book practices what it preaches: succinct, specific, engaging writing.*

Now cut the number in half. Free of that fat, your copy will hit more powerfully—and penetrate your prospect's resistance.

Now, cut it in half again.

If you cannot describe what makes you different and excellent in twenty-five words or less, don't fix your copy. Fix your company.

Shorter Sells

In 1992 a thirty-one-year-old Minneapolis executive, frustrated that the companies for whom he wanted to work weren't calling him back, retained an expert résumé writer.

The writer quickly detected a problem. It was not the fellow's credentials. It was his résumé. It managed to stretch just nine years of work into three copy-filled pages. The writer knew that some recipients of the résumé refused the ordeal of reading the manuscript, and others were putting it down before the strong ending.

> *"Great jazz musicians know when not to play the note. They know where to leave the space."*
> *—Rick Joy, architect and Harvard teacher*

Two weeks later, the executive sent his now revised, one-page résumé to his two favorite target employers. Both responded immediately.

Three weeks later, the Young Turk got the job.

Respect clients' time—especially in communicating.

How to Read a Sentence

Many of America's grocery stores recently ran an in-store promotion for Agfa film. To ensure the promotion's success, the staff placed large posters touting the film near each store's entrance. Then they braced for the rush.

No rush. Not even a jog.

The poster read, "Agfa film is among the premier color films available on the market today."

The poster said nothing. Edit this statement to its essence. First, delete the last five words, because they mean nothing. If the grocery is promoting Agfa, that film must be available on the market today.

If Agfa is *the* premier color film, the author certainly would say that. But apparently it ranks only among the premier films. Shoppers can find other premier films, perhaps many. So Agfa is merely *a* premier color film.

So, this poster actually said, "Agfa is a premier color film." That's it, that's all.

That's Agfa's compelling sales pitch. If the people who approved these posters had read carefully, they would have sent the writer back to find more compelling prose.

The author of this ad knew that she had nothing to say. So she hit the Writer's Default Button—the one that always pops out a cliché. She tried to bolster her claim for Agfa film by adding that favorite—but meaningless—phrase "available on the market today."

The poster lacks power. People who read the

poster respond, "Who says Agfa is premier? And if the film is so special, why does this poster sound so ordinary?"

The author should have replaced her puffery with a fact: Agfa recently was ranked one of the world's three best color films by America's three leading photography publications. Or she might have mentioned the number of prize-winning photographers who use Agfa film. Or something. Anything.

Read your sentences ruthlessly. Make sure each says something concrete that people will believe. Make sure you would believe them, and that each is backed by evidence.

Cut until only the truth, powerfully told, remains. Then ask: Are there even more powerful truths that we can tell?

Cut all the fat. Then ask: Does the muscle that remains have power?

Your Final Step: The Frenchman-on-the-Street Test

A French mathematician devised the first rule of communicating: "A theory is not complete until you can explain it to the first person you meet on the street."

The appeal of your key message—the description

of what you do, your key point of difference, and the benefit of your point of difference—should resonate with everyone. Unless everyone can understand your message, too few people will.

Edit your message until everyone understands it.

Absolute Brilliance

It's a cultural smorgasbord: born in Sweden, England, New York, and South Africa, and inspired by a classic American sitcom. And while it may seem too old—almost twenty-five—and too global to be relevant to most businesses, it stands alone.

You can find no better model for your advertising.

It started, as many businesses do, with envy. In 1978 several Swedish entrepreneurs decided that if the Finns could sell vodka to Americans, so could the Swedes. Three years later the entrepreneurs asked TBWA in New York to launch their new vodka. Two relative newcomers received the job: Geoff Hayes, a South African writer, and Graham Turner, an art director from England.

The pair quickly generated two campaigns. The first was a throwaway that played on Sweden's cold winters and hardy natives. The second began with an image that had struck Hayes during a *Honeymooners* rerun. Hayes envisioned a vodka bottle with a halo floating over it. Below that image, Hayes had written the headline:

"Absolut. It's perfectly wonderful."

It seemed almost right. Hayes showed it to Turner, who saw a simpler message. "What about 'Absolute Perfection'?"

Perfect was right.

Twenty years after Hayes and Turner's brainstorm, a SoHo antique shop still sells copies of old Absolut ads. One advertising industry group has placed the campaign, with just two others—Volkswagen and Nike—in its Hall of Fame.

What makes these ads so effective?

First, they aren't ads. They're a *campaign*. The Absolut campaign repeats one idea, each ad so fresh that readers look forward to the next.

The campaign is *brand-based*. If you remember nothing else you remember "Absolut."

The ads ensure that you remember the product by giving you almost nothing else to think about. The campaign is *simple*. Three words—like "Absolut San Francisco," for example. A single arresting visual. No copy.

You also remember another key element: that distinctive bottle. Before Absolut, most liquor came in long-necked, square-shouldered bottles. Demonstrating the power of opposites in marketing, the Swedes designed their bottle with a short neck and round shoulders.

As a result, every Absolut ad conveys two unique traits of the brand—its name and distinctive packaging—which multiplies the effectiveness of each ad.

The campaign is *proprietary*. It looks like no one

else's; it could be no one else's. Only Absolut can say "absolut" and incorporate that shape.

The campaign recognizes that people don't believe what marketers say; people believe what they decide for themselves. So the campaign only *implies*. By doing this, the ads make readers decide that Absolut is like them: sophisticated yet not stuffy, successful yet hip.

The campaign is *visual*. It arrests the eye. Why is the bottle under lock and key? Why the halo? Or most fun of all, where *is* that bottle—Oh There It Is! (In one particularly deft ad, the artist meticulously altered an aerial photo of Central Park in the shape of an Absolut bottle.)

Not least of all, the campaign is *different*—so different that two years after it started, several Absolut executives still wanted it killed. "Too cutesy," one complained. Like many great names,

> *This point—that people believe what they decide rather than what they are told—is critical to understanding persuasion. If a marketer makes an explicit claim—"the world's best vodka"—people tend to dismiss it. If the same marketers provide the material from which people can draw that conclusion themselves, they believe it; quite naturally, we believe our own conclusions. Mathematician Blaise Pascal made exactly this point: "We are generally more persuaded by the reasons we discover ourselves than by those given to us by others."*

offices, and ads, Absolut's campaign invites criticism. It should say more, some will argue, or take its product more seriously.

The campaign transformed Absolut into something

it's not: great. (In blind taste tests it receives average scores.) More remarkably, the campaign took a liquor that U.S. law requires to be without distinctive character, aroma, taste, or color and made it distinctive, unique, warm, and witty—and allowed the company to charge more for every bottle.

This cultural smorgasbord demonstrates advertising at its most powerful and provides a model for anyone marketing anything.

Be like Absolut: simple, visual, implicit, proprietary, different, and brand-obsessive.

THE VELVET
SLEDGEHAMMER

A Compelling Message

KEY TREND:
THE DECLINE OF TRUST

1919   Eight members of the Chicago White Sox throw the World Series in exchange for money from gamblers. Deceit meets America's national pastime.

1920–29   The muckrakers: Sinclair Lewis exposes phony evangelists, Ida Tarbell exposes the Rockefellers, and everyone exposes evil businessmen and corrupt politicians.

1959   Appearing before the House Committee on Interstate and Foreign Commerce, Columbia University professor Charles Van Doren admits to participating in fixing the hit NBC quiz show Twenty-One. *We can't trust professors, either.*

1961   Burt Lancaster wins the Academy Award for his portrayal of an amoral evangelist in Elmer Gantry, *based on the Sinclair Lewis book.*

1965   Thirty-one-year-old Ralph Nader, a fan since childhood of Ida Tarbell and Sinclair Lewis, attacks General Motors in his book Unsafe at Any Speed: The Designed-in Dangers of the American Automobile. *General Motors compounds its problem by invading Nader's privacy to find information with which to discredit the author.*

July 19, 1972   Americans learn that a Republican security aide is among the five men arrested two days earlier for breaking into the Democratic National Committee headquarters in the Watergate hotel and office complex.

August 8, 1974   Impeached for his attempt to hide his administration's role in the Watergate break-in, Richard Nixon becomes America's first president to resign.

1982   Janet Cooke is fired from the Washington Post *after admitting that her 1982 Pulitzer Prize–winning story on drug use included a totally fabricated story. Further investigation reveals that Cooke also fabricated her Vassar and Sorbonne educations and fluency in four languages. She is discovered twenty years later selling Liz Claiborne in a Kalamazoo, Michigan, department store. In an Only-in-America twist, her discoverer learns that Cooke has sold the movie rights to her story for more than $1 million.*

1982   John DeLorean, a former top General Motors executive, is indicted for money laundering to raise money for his new car company.

1989   Praise the Lord and pass the $20 million: Jim Bakker, who earlier confessed to an affair with church secretary Jessica Hahn, is sentenced to five years in prison for defrauding members of the Praise the Lord ministry of $158 million.

1990   Michael Milken, of the once well-regarded financial firm Drexel Burnham Lambert, pleads guilty and is sentenced to ten years in prison for securities fraud and racketeering in the sales of "junk bonds." Recognizing the harm to its name, his firm ceases operating as Drexel Burnham Lambert.

1995–2000   In defending a federal class action suit against them, tobacco company executives testify they did not know that smoking cigarettes could be harmful.

2002   Enron and Arthur Andersen. The likely beginning on an era of distrusting huge companies.

In *The Search for Signs of Intelligent Life in the Universe,* Lily Tomlin offers an understandable reaction to the last fifty years:

"I worry that no matter how cynical you become," she says, "you still can't keep up."

We do not know who to trust.

In the 1970s, millions of Americans hitchhiked. The

A detailed analysis of the apparent decline of trust in America can be found in Robert Putnam's Bowling Alone: The Collapse and Revival of American Community.

biggest challenge was not the risk—no one felt any—but other hitchhikers, with whom they competed for rides. Today, no one dares enter a stranger's car. Hitchhiking is less popular than whaling.

We disbelieve our newspapers, our priests and preachers, and our political and business leaders—and one another. Fifty-five percent of Americans in 1960 agreed that "most people can be trusted." By 2000 only 34 percent did.

This feeling has evolved from the baby boomers' famous warning, "Never trust anyone over thirty" to the bumper sticker "Question Authority" to the even broader "Who can you trust?"

"A generation is coming of age in America that doesn't take the news straight, that doesn't take the utterances of public figures straight, that doesn't take social games straight. . . . It sees giant con games everywhere."
      —*Jacob Brackman,* The Put-On (1971)

We even disbelieve our own "knowledge." Read the best-known thinkers of the Enlightenment, writing a little over two centuries ago, and you feel amazed by their confidence. They saw a Newtonian world that worked like a machine. Understand the moving parts and you could predict everything. Mankind was about to control the world.

Today, our world looks neither controllable nor predictable; it looks chaotic. Chaos theory fills the shelves of our bookstores and, with the popular book and movie *Jurassic Park,* enters our mainstream.

We feel uncertain—including about others. But because we feel we can trust fewer people, we value those we trust even more; they are more rare and therefore more valuable. We love the assurance they provide, that there is someone we can rely on in this chaotic world.

Our choices—both their sheer number and type—add to our uncertainty. We cannot see or inspect much of what we buy. Estée Lauder, the woman behind the famous perfumes, expressed our problems with intangibles when she observed, "If a person cannot smell it, a salesperson cannot sell it."

Our senses help us tell if something is right. But how do you smell, taste, touch, or hear a service? What sense can you rely on to determine if you have chosen the right doctor, consulting engineers, or bank?

You worry, What if the service fails? Does the firm offer a warranty or a full refund? Services rarely do, and often can't. You cannot return a bad haircut, knee surgery, or catered party.

Fear, uncertainty, doubt—marketers first noticed this trio of feelings among prospects for computers and software, and dubbed it the "FUD Factor." Today, FUD dominates everything. Clients are fearful, uncertain, and doubtful. *But*.

Like all problems, this presents you with an opportunity. The ability to inspire trust has become more rare, and as a result, more valuable—particularly if you explore the recommendations that follow.

Cole's Wisdom

"Trust in Allah, but tie your camel."
                                        —Arab proverb

From the mouths of babes come marketing gems.

This one came just after Christmas 1999. My five-year-old son, Cole, and I were driving into a parking spot at our neighborhood Barnes & Noble. Cole noticed a sign in a window next to the bookstore, and read it aloud from the backseat.

"Special . . . Sale . . . This . . . Week . . . Only!" Cole wasn't buying.

"They're just trying to get you to come in and buy stuff," he said. "It's really not special."

Five years old.

At five, Cole decided that you can't trust businesses or believe their ads. "Special," "Sale," or "This week only!" are just words.

Cole is today's customer. He thinks you'll say anything to sell anything. You are shouting at skeptics.

You must sell more honestly and believably than ever—just to get an audience.

Say only what people will believe; they will appreciate your honesty and modesty, and begin to trust you.

Honesty is the best tactic.

The Faster Way to Be Believed

Admit a weakness.

People who reveal something negative about their service win more business. Psychologists insist this can be easily explained. We assume that people who reveal a weakness are inclined to tell only the truth—even when it hurts them. We can trust those people.

Revealing a weakness also charms and disarms a prospect, and helps establish the common ground upon which good relationships are built.

Unselling often is the best strategy.

A Wolverine and the Comfort Principle

How do prospects choose?

To unlock one key, let's look at one prospect—Adam Stenavich—and how he chose his college.

Research suggests that students considering colleges are most influenced by their parents' recommendations. After that, the strongest influences are the university's reputation, its campus, and its proximity to the student's home; almost nine in ten college students attend a college within 150 miles of their parents' home.

Research tells us that. Listening tells us more.

Consider young Mr. Stenavich of Marshfield, Wisconsin. By the end of his junior year in June 2000, his six-foot-six and 260-pound frame had caught the attention of college football recruiters. Because he wanted to stay near home and play for a strong team, Adam quickly narrowed his choices to two: the University of Wisconsin, whose team had recently won the Rose Bowl, and the University of Michigan, a perennial top-twenty team.

The odds favored Wisconsin, the closer school. Adam chose Michigan.

Was it his parents' influence? Not at all. They preferred Wisconsin.

Did Michigan's fine academic reputation break the tie? No. Adam considered the schools to be academic equals.

Then why Michigan, the more distant school?

"I got to meet the players," Adam said.

Michigan's reputation, campus, and football team got the Wolverines into the finals. But like prospects for every service, Adam did not choose the school. *He chose the relationship.* He met and liked the players. They connected.

The basics get you into the game. Then relationships take over, in every service from colleges to chiropractors.

Cultivate your—and all your people's—relationship skills.

What the Best Salespeople Sell (in order)

Themselves.

Their company.

Their service or product.

Price.

Sell yourself first.

What Ordinary Salespeople Sell (in order)

Price.
   Their service or product.
   Themselves.
   Their company.
   Sell your price last.

How to Read a Short List

In the summer of 2000, O.J. Oshinowo of Naperville, Illinois, had narrowed his list of colleges to five: Purdue, Illinois, Georgia Tech, Northwestern, and Stanford.

Like all short lists, O.J.'s communicated useful information to each contender: his perceptions, biases, and fears.

O.J.'s list reveals at least three things:

1. He wants to become an engineer. All five schools are known for engineering. (The contenders also might assume that O.J. is specifically interested in electrical engineering, because *U.S. News & World Report* ranked Purdue and Georgia Tech first and second in that discipline.)

2. He prefers a competitive football team, but not a

dominant one—an accurate description of all five schools.

3. If two schools seem equal, he will prefer the school closer to home. Three of his top five schools are within a day's drive of Naperville.

Seeing this short list, Stanford's recruiters should have felt optimistic that summer. Their school's engineering program ranks behind only MIT's—which has no football team—and their team had played in the Rose Bowl just six months before. And unlike many prospects, O.J.'s inclusion of two schools far from Naperville suggested he is willing to leave the Midwest. Stanford's recruiters should realize that if they can answer O.J.'s concerns about the distance to Palo Alto, they could win this marketing battle.

Like most prospects' lists, Oshinowo's tells these finalists how to position themselves. Northwestern, the school nearest to Naperville, must emphasize the advantages of proximity. Stanford must overcome them. Better yet, Stanford's recruiters should do what every good presenter does. They should go beyond neutralizing their disadvantage and turn it into an asset.

They can do this by videotaping current Stanford students from Illinois, describing their experiences, the value of seeing a different part of Amer-

> *Oshinowo's final decision revealed even more about the attractions between services and prospects. Oshinowo was prepared to sign with Northwestern, in closer-by Evanston, Illinois. But Oshinowo chose Stanford, and mentioned one of its biggest draws: One of its top electrical engineering professors was, like Oshinowo, a native of Nigeria.*

ica, and the sheer coolness of the San Francisco Bay Area.

Your prospect's short list reveals his preferences and his perceptions of you and your competitors.

Does your prospect's list suggest a bias for firms with experience in your category, for example?

Does the prospect favor the "brand names"?

Does the list suggest he is relying on one or more firms' past reputation? After seeing Oshinowo's list, for example, the Stanford recruiters might worry that he believes all five schools have strong engineering programs, when only four do. You must educate these less-informed prospects about your industry and try to stretch out the selection process, to increase the chances they will learn the truth.

What are they looking for?

What are they afraid of?

What do they see as your strength and weakness? (If, for example, the prospect is interviewing four fairly large firms and your small one, they're revealing that they prefer large firms but will consider a small one. From that you can ask, What does this prospect like about larger firms? What large-firm traits and skills does our firm have?)

This study also can tell you whether to proceed any further—or save yourself the time and expense of a mere show. If four of the five firms, for example, are similar to one another but different from you, the prospect may already be sold on their shared trait; the prospect is inviting you out of courtesy or curiosity. If four of Oshinowo's schools were within a day's drive of Naperville, for example, Stanford should consider

pulling back and spending its limited time and resources on better prospects.

*Study every short list. They're longer on infor-
mation than you think.*

How to Read a Short List, Two

Before any presentation, draw up a list of your competitors.

Beside each firm's name, write how your prospect
would describe each firm in one positive word and
one negative word. This chart tells you how to position yourself in the pitch.

It tells you three key things.

1. How does the prospect see you and your competitors? You must accept their perception, however
erroneous.

2. What do they see as your possible weakness?
Shore up this weakness.

3. What are your competitors' perceived strengths?
A key step: *Prepare to undermine these perceived
strengths and reposition them as weaknesses.*

If your competitor is a specialist and you are not,
for example, stress the value of working with a generalist in this particular situation.

Know your competitors' positions and use your position as your theme. Open and close your presentation with that theme, supported by powerful and credible reasons the prospect should choose you.

Position yourself in every presentation. Studying your prospect's short list will help you.

Wield a Velvet Sledgehammer

Alec Baldwin offered Jack Lemmon and several other terrified salesmen some typical selling advice in the movie *Glengarry Glen Ross*.

"The key is ABC, gentlemen.

"Always . . . Be . . . Closing."

Baldwin's classic advice may apply to products. But

A good example of repositioning a competitor's strength as a weakness: Many state agencies are required by their state's laws to solicit bids and hear presentations for their outsourced business—legal, accounting, consulting, and advertising services, for example—at specified intervals. The firm currently handling that business usually is invited and often is the overwhelming favorite—if only because it is the devil that the state agency knows. The incumbent naturally stresses as its strength its long experience working with the agency. The competing firms should express a respect for the incumbent and its work already done and an intent to build on that work, but improve it from a new and fresh perspective. The competitors should transform the incumbent's apparent strength into a weakness.

if you are selling the staple of the New Economy—services—forget ABC.

Products are things made by someone else; product salespeople merely act as go-betweens. They can gush, "Isn't this a beauty?" or "Isn't this amazing?" without offending the prospect. They are merely gushing over a car made by some gifted Germans.

Now change what the salespeople are selling from a red German convertible to a service—let's say IT consulting. What if they pitch the same way they pitched the car? What if they say "Our firm is amazing—the best in the region"?

Raving about a car is acceptable and understandable: Many cars, pens, and scarves, to name just three products, are worth raving about. When you gush about your firm's services, however, you are doing something different:

You are bragging.

To hard-sell and "always be closing," you must gush and rave. When it's your services you are selling, raving sounds boastful—and not even braggarts like other braggarts.

Clients prize humility—reason enough to never hard sell again. Go softly and slowly.

Sell soft.

> *Services often sell too hard in their advertising, and leap the fine line between touting and bragging. The University of Pennsylvania's outstanding business school, Wharton, recently waged a campaign to attract students. Its headline proclaimed, "At Wharton, we don't teach the rules of business. We write them." Among other flaws, the ad manages to make one of America's most prestigious schools sound like an upstart outsider, shouting to be heard.*

A Game of Give and Take

The Supremes once offered some good advice about selling. "You can't hurry love. You just have to wait."

You cannot hurry a relationship. And because selling today involves selling a relationship, you cannot hurry the sale of service.

You just have to wait.

Hurry the sale and you may gain a sale but lose a customer. The reason comes from the study of strong relationships: The reason is boundaries.

Two people achieve a strong relationship by reaching beyond the boundaries they usually maintain between themselves and strangers. Each party, however, moves beyond his or her boundary and into another person's life only with the other's consent, always recognizing the other person's separateness and boundaries. Even together, people must remain separate to thrive.

The hard sale violates this rule. The hard seller rushes in, ignoring the need for consent, and plows through the other's boundary. "Forget it. I have a quota to make." This won't work. The prospect feels violated—because his boundaries have been.

Sell slow.

Why Hard Selling Has Gotten Harder

A leading American outsourcing firm recently presented two revealing sales figures at its annual meeting.

Line one, 1998: 17 percent increase in new clients acquired.

Line two, 1999: 19 percent increase in clients lost.

These two figures were intertwined. An alarming number of the clients lost were the ones the firm had acquired the year before. They acquired them by goading their salespeople to sell more aggressively. Like most hard sold clients, those newly acquired clients felt pushed into the sale and expected what hard sellers always promise: the moon. When the company delivered less, the disappointed clients fled.

These clients did not actually buy initially. They surrendered; giving in was easier than saying no. It meant the phone call barrage would end and they could return to some relative calm.

The victims of hard selling rarely become lasting clients—in part because they felt pushed from the start. At their first opportunity, they will switch providers.

The damage grows. These former clients often criticize the firm to others, which shrinks the firm's pool of prospects.

Hard selling shrinks your market.

The final hard sale scorecard: one short-term customer gained, one long-term and several future clients lost: a net loss.

Forget cutting to the close. Assure prospects that your service offers genuine value but that you understand that decisions take time. Respect those prospects' needs and boundaries. Periodically remind them that you're interested and available if they need more information.

In short, treat business relationships like personal ones: Give them time and space to grow.

And one more thought: If you wonder if you're pushing a prospect too hard, you are.

Hard sales lose business.

What Would Aesop and Jesus Do?

"Tell me a story, Daddy."

Is there a more familiar request in any language?

Why are children so obsessed with stories that "story" is among the first words they learn? Because stories help humans understand ideas.

Aesop and Jesus must have known instinctively what a well-regarded professor of neurophysiology recently offered: that the oldest hardwired neural pathway in the human brain is for stories. When each man wanted to teach moral and ethical lessons, he chose stories as his tool—Aesop told fables while Jesus offered parables.

Stories dominate our lives. They dominate every entertainment form: novels and nonfiction, movies and plays, even dance and music. "Candle in the Wind" was Elton John's poignant telling of the brief life story of Marilyn Monroe, and later, of Lady Diana. Our evening news repeats story after story, as Garret Morris on *Saturday Night Live* reminded us with his introduction to the news for the hearing-impaired, bellowing "OUR TOP STORY TONIGHT!"

Children and adults love stories. As children we hide under sheets with flashlights because we must find out that night how the story ends. As adults you walk through the aisles of planes and see fifty people reading; forty are reading novels, while the others are reading stories in books and magazines.

Stories help people get it; they hear, and they *see*.

Stories also reach places that no description can: people's hearts. Consider, for example, the many attempts to define "love." One author devised one popular definition, calling love "unconditional positive regard."

Now doesn't that capture love in its entire splendor? No, just as the best way to describe your firm's special qualities is not through mere claims and descriptions like "customer-centered," but with stories that vividly capture those qualities.

Help your prospects understand by giving them what they love: stories.

Perfect your storytelling.

Lessons from Colorado: Find the Force

The partners at Go.edu in Westminster, Colorado, felt stalled.

For months the foursome had been trying to sell their consulting services to a Colorado school district. What are we doing wrong, they asked each other. "Are we saying something wrong?"

Their problem was typical: They were saying the right thing to the wrong person. Their contact had no power in her organization. In fact, she lacked credibility with other district executives. Her peers actually regarded her championing of Go.edu as evidence the firm was weak.

Like millions of salespeople on their phones right now, Go.edu had chosen the wrong person. They were not reaching The Force.

In selling your services, get aligned with The Force—the person with the influence, power, and inclination to act. Before you approach a prospective client, determine who has the influence, can get a decision made, and can get it made quickly enough to make your prospecting profitable and satisfying.

If you enter a firm through a weak person, you will be weakened by your association with them, and kill your deal before you can propose it.

Find The Force before you sell.

What Your Prospects'
Nods Mean

An experienced Merrill Lynch representative sched-
uled a meeting with a client couple. His agenda con-
tained one line: Sell the couple an investment for their
recent windfall.

The adviser, W.H., felt blessed by this couple because they understood investing. The wife was a CPA,
an MBA, and a former associate at Peat Marwick. The
husband advised several major investment firms and
studied investing.

W.H. knew these clients would like his recommendations—a fund that specialized in European companies in growth industries such as information
technology and telecommunications.

W.H. delivered his well-rehearsed pitch. The couple nodded several times. At the end they thanked
W.H., said they'd study his recommendation, and
waved as W.H. left their driveway. He was beaming;
he thought he'd made the sale. But while W.H. was
clicking his heels, his clients were scratching their
heads.

"What did he say?" the husband asked his CPA/
MBA wife.

"I don't know, I thought you understood—you
were nodding."

"So were you!"

Each partner had nodded because they did not
want to appear stupid. They figured W.H. had given

his spiel to dozens of prospects, all of whom must have understood it. The couple did not want to appear foolish. So they nodded.

This scene from W.H. and the Nodders is playing everywhere right now: millions of sellers, millions of nodders.

When your prospects nod, they often don't understand. Stop and clarify. Then go back after your presentation and remove every rough edge.

If a prospect nods, stop.

Why Cold Calls Leave People Cold

I have never heard of you.

You are calling me at work.

You are interrupting me.

How did you get my number?

Are things so bad you have to call strangers to get business?

Why should I buy something from someone I've never heard of?

People feel most comfortable with companies they think they know—and mistrust ones they've never heard of. You must get known.

Get out, mingle, meet. Ignore Groucho Marx's policy of never joining a club that would allow him as a member; join a club. (But never take up an activity or join a club in which you are not truly interested. You will lack affinity with the other participants—a key to a lasting relationship.)

Warm every call—somehow.

Sell Like You Date

You are a woman, your phone rings. You answer to hear this remarkable request.

"Hi, you don't know me, but I'm David. Want to go out for lunch?"

Does that cold call work?

A service is a relationship between a provider and a recipient. Given that, what are you actually doing when you cold call to sell a service? You are inviting a stranger to have a relationship with you.

What are the odds this will work?

Cold calls cause cold shoulders.

Why Goldman Sachs Cannot Cold Call

Goldman Sachs doesn't cold call. Nor do Kleiner Perkins, State Farm, Russell Reynolds, and Merck.

They can't. Their good names warm every call they make.

Their marketing has made their name so familiar that people answer their calls. When Goldman Sachs calls, people listen.

This suggests a key test: Is your marketing working so well that it warms every sales call?

If not, revise your marketing. While you are doing that, call only the prospects you already have warmed.

Good marketing eliminates cold calls.

Remember Eddie Haskell

Your audience includes four people: the Top Dog and three associates.

Who should you address? Who must you win over?

The associates. The Top Dog knows she is Top Dog and doesn't need reminding. Her associates, however, feel like subordinates. If they are typical subordinates, they think they deserve their boss's title and the fawning that goes with it.

Because associates are sensitive to any hint you consider them underlings, you must make each one feel important. Address the boss too often and everyone—the associates *and* the boss—will decide you are a shameless bootlicker.

We love people who respect us as equals; we hate

toadies and sycophants—which is why *Leave It to Beaver's* Eddie Haskell made a perfect villain.

If you think of your prospect's subordinates as subordinates, pack your portfolios and head back to your office. Instead, reverse your view of your audience.

Treat associates like bosses and bosses like associates.

A Trick to Improve Your Presentations

"And now and with great pride I introduce our speaker—though she needs no introduction. Her brilliant career includes . . ." Why do most speeches begin this way?

Because this introduction works. The introducer assures you the speaker is brilliant. Then you hear her, and she is brilliant—not because she is, but because the introducer coaxed you into believing it.

This is another example of a placebo effect. You experience what you expect to experience. The introduction made you expect brilliance, and so you heard it—*even if you didn't.*

Capitalize on this effect.

The day before your presentation, send each prospect a summary of your presenter's background that creates the perception that "this person is really good." To be sure your audience "hears" this introduction, place in front of each audience member a brief agenda with a short biography of each presenter. To ensure that every member reads it, if only to pass time before your presentation, make sure this agenda is the only item in front of each member.

Do for your presenters what smart introducers do for keynote speakers: Create a great expectation.

Sell your presenters before you present.

L.A. Confidential and the Rule of Contact

An interviewer asked movie producer Arnon Milchan how director Curtis Hanson convinced him to produce _L.A. Confidential,_ which became a 1998 Best Picture nominee. What was it about the story?

It was more than the story.

"Before you hear the story," Milchan said, "you look in the director's eyes. The look I got from Curtis was the look of passion—and decency."

Since the Greeks, we have believed that eyes reveal our souls. We assume that someone who refuses to make eye contact is hiding something—and we probably are right. Studies continually show that people avert their eyes from listeners when they lie.

Your eye contact engages the audience and helps them trust you and your message. Anything that breaks that contact so long that you must regain that trust reduces your odds of success.

To avoid breaking contact, use visual aids only for transitions or to illustrate critical points. Otherwise, keep eye contact. It builds trust.

Use visual aids sparingly.

Lincoln Had No Slides at Gettysburg

Galactic Inc. believes it is dazzling its prospect with slide after slide that highlights Galactic's excellence.

The lights go on. The prospect praises Galactic's work and insight and promises to call Galactic soon. Two days later the prospect calls.

> *"Ever since we outlawed PowerPoint several years ago, our stock has shot up."*
> —Scott McNealy, founder and CEO,
> Sun Microsystems

Merely Global got the business.

Galactic's presenters did not know that bullet points deserve their name: Their bullets killed them. How?

Because whatever you sell, you do not sell things; today, not even products are products. They are solutions preceded by a service—advice—and followed by other services, including support. This means that you are not selling slides, although some companies' obsession with PowerPoint might suggest otherwise. You are selling the people clicking the slides.

This dictates that the key in presenting is not presenting your *ideas* well. It is presenting your *people* well.

When prospects gaze at slides, they are not looking at what you are selling: you. If you darken the room for dramatic effect, your problem only grows more dramatic. Now your prospects are not looking into your eyes—where relationships are made—*and* they are not listening to you. They are reading.

Naturally, you can jolt them from this dangerous practice. Just say something that does not appear on your slide.

But this makes them flinch. They wonder if they understood your slide, because the point you are verbalizing sounds different from the one they read. They feel disconnected, distracted, and uncomfortable—a virtually unsellable prospect.

You must look into their eyes.

The rules of evidence reflect this point. The rule against hearsay forbids a party from admitting into evidence a statement made by someone outside the courtroom. That person must appear in front of the jurors, because the law also believes our eyes are windows to our soul. The jurors must be able to look the person making the statement in the eyes, to gauge whether that person is credible and sincere.

Your prospects must, too. So use slides only to illustrate a point that you cannot express as well in words. Otherwise, make contact.

Prospects cannot choose in the dark.

How to Boost Your Chances

A legendary Big Ten coach once said three things can happen when you pass a football, and two are bad. The same principle applies to presentations.

Only one thing can go wrong when you present without slides: You forget what you planned to say next. If that happens, you can glance down at your outline and start again. Easy and harmless.

What if you present and the wrong slide, or no slide, comes up?

What happens?

Everything stops. The speaker starts fidgeting because he isn't certain how to fix it. He makes a weak joke about technology. The listeners, who had been watching attentively, slump back in their seats. The speaker fusses while the audience members peek at their watches, stare at the ceiling, and wonder.

Shouldn't the bugs be out of this presentation by now?

Didn't these folks rehearse?

Can't they afford good equipment?

And if they can't present, what else can't they do?

Cut your slides. It will cut your risks.

Impressive Slide Shows Aren't

"We've got to do a bunch of slides," the account executive insists. "All those slides will impress this prospect."

No they won't. Thirty slides do not convey how much you know. They suggest you have so little command over your material that you need thirty slides to prompt you.

The people who earn their prospect's confidence need neither slides nor notes. Their notes are stored in their heads for quick, impressive access.

To impress a prospect, don't read. Speak.

Remember: It's a *Visual* Aid

We call them visual aids. They *aid* people in making a point. And they are *visual*—they exist to say a thousand words, because no audience member can read that many.

A slide filled only with words is neither visual nor an aid. It does not aid you in communicating; it only distracts your audience. It makes people in your audience wonder if they should listen or just read.

Most people can't resist looking at a slide when it's flashed on. So they look. And when they are looking at a slide they are not looking at you—and usually not listening, either.

Put two dozen words on a screen and your audience will read them while they ignore you. If you use a simple image instead—a photo of the Eiffel Tower, for example, to emphasize your company's experience in Europe—the audience, with nothing to read, will listen to you.

The simple image provides an attractive and relevant background, and gives them nothing to distract them from what they are buying:

You.

If you must use visual aids, use "visual" visual aids.

Packaging the Bold or Conservative Idea

Even radicals are conservative—particularly about their jobs and their bank accounts.

So how do you sell a novel idea?

Make it seem less radical. Dress conservatively: dark suit, well-shined sensible shoes, crisp solid shirt or blouse, no extra jewelry.

When architect Michael Graves in 1980 presented his audacious idea for Portland, Oregon's, new city offices, he appeared wearing the preferred attire of

Portland's conservative city leaders: a Harris tweed jacket.

If you fear the idea you will present may seem too conservative, do the reverse. Be bolder. Wear a brightly colored item and an unusual watch, for example. (An M&Co. watch, particularly its "commuter watch" with the 12 appearing where the 3 should be, almost always get noticed.) Package yourself to reassure them your firm is creative, but intentionally and for sound reasons chose this more conservative solution.

Package bold ideas conservatively and conservative ideas boldly.

Do Like the Romans

Birds of a feather do business together. Prospects choose service providers who share their tastes.

Hence, an often violated rule of presenting: Dress like your audience, but just a bit better.

The "better" conveys that your presentation is important—and that *they* are, too. The "like" communicates that you are like them and puts you more at ease, something audiences always sense. And by not overdressing, you assure your prospects that you're not trying to pull cashmere over their eyes.

"But I call on farmers," a financial planner from Iowa says. "A suit will put these clients off." Clothing does not put people off; pretentious clothing does.

We dislike people who affect superiority, who dress to boast, intimidate, or put us in our place. That message never sells, whether you deliver it with words or clothes.

Should you change clothes before driving to the farm? Not to assume the role of a farmer. Doing that is as pretentious as dressing like Donald Trump. (Remember that "pretentious" comes from the word "pretend," to act like someone you are not.)

A Los Angeles public relations agent for Quaker Oats once demonstrated this principle, that dressing down can be as off-putting as dressing up. Assigned to persuade an Oregon running club to co-sponsor a race in Portland in 1987, he purchased the classic Pacific Northwest style: a Pendleton wool shirt. When he presented in Portland several days later, the Oregonians could not fail to notice the fresh-from-the-box creases on his shirt, and how incongruous it looked with a $45 razor cut and gold aviator glasses.

Mr. I'm-Just-Like-You's presentation fell on dumbfounded ears.

Dress honestly and a little up.

Keep Talking Happy Talk

People shoot messengers.

Beware of saying anything that might be perceived as negative. You're selling a feeling. You've succeeded if your audience leaves feeling good.

Never threaten that spirit. Never criticize the room, the weather, last night's performance by the local team—nothing. Negatives pollute the room's air and brand you as negative, too.

Shakespeare got it right more than four hundred years ago:

"It is never good to bring bad news."

Accentuate the positive, avoid the negative.

Dion and the Rule of Three

When the rock singer Dion decided to salute four American leaders who died young, he did not call his song *Abraham, Martin, John, and Bobby.* He dropped Bobby.

Dion understood the Rule of Three.

People easily remember the Father, Son, and Holy Ghost. They remember the Three Musketeers and the Three Pigs, Bears, and Blind Mice. Not to mention the Atchison, Topeka, and Santa Fe; Winken, Blinken, and Nod; and Peter, Paul, and Mary.

The Stooges wisely stopped at three but the Marx Brothers didn't. They originally had a fourth and what happened? Most movie buffs can name Groucho, Harp, and Chico, but can't remember Zeppo (or even that there was a fifth Marx brother, Gummo).

Try remembering the Seven Dwarfs. Most people quickly get Sleepy and Dopey, then pause and puzzle. Depending on their temperament, they can remember Happy or Grumpy. Then they start searching the skies for the other names; too many names.

People who see a slide with four points subconsciously know that they cannot process all that information. So they pay little attention—and miss all four points.

Your audience feels overloaded when they enter the room—work to be done, errands to run, e-mails to answer.

If you must use slides, don't stuff them.

Edit each slide to three lines, then each line to three words. This encourages discipline, makes you focus on your stronger points, makes your message more forceful, and gives the audience more time and reason to look at you.

Doubt this? Look at this bullet point from a recent Fortune 100 company's presentation:

- Increase sales to 125% of 2000 levels

Now look at this bullet, which says the same thing:

- Sell 25% more

Three points, three words each.
(P.S. Doc, Sneezy and Bashful.)

Think Pterodactyls and Typhoons

Driving along the highway, the road looks familiar. You start to tire and lose concentration. Suddenly something jolts you awake: a billboard reading,

> Friendly Pterodactyls, 1 Mile.
> (Bring Bird Seed. *Lots*.)

Unusual words do that. They break the monotony and demand attention. Your presentations must do this, too. Review your material and look for opportunities to replace common words with uncommon ones.

Consider this typical slide at a brokerage's recent investor presentation:

"Forecast for the Next Quarter."

You've been there and read that. You start to drift off. Now imagine that message with a less common expression:

"The Next Quarter: Storms Ahead?"

Much better—as the wide eyes in your audience would tell you. They would open even more, though, if you kept editing. "Storm," for example, is ambiguous and humdrum. How about a more specific and dramatic expression?

"The Quarter Ahead: Hurricane Approaching?"

Better, but keep going:

"The Quarter Ahead: Typhoon Coming?"

"Typhoon" works better because the word is used less often than hurricane. Typhoons are hurricanes that originate in the Pacific Ocean. "Typhoon" also grabs your attention because of its sound—the same phenomenon that makes people smile when they hear "boob," "loon," or "kazoo."

(Hint: To find uncommon words, try WordNet at cogsci.princeton.edu. Type in a conventional word and WordNet will show you several more interesting ones.)

Seek out uncommon ways to say common things.

BLUE MARTINIS AND OMAHA SURFING

A Reassuring Brand

Key Trend: The Rise of Invisibles and Intangibles

He sold hydraulic machinery—or so he thought.

He described his business to me as we flew to Philadelphia, punctuating his remarks with shakes of his head, amazed by the changes. I had to ask:

What is your business? Is it selling hydraulics?

No. Nobody buys the hydraulics. Everybody makes good hydraulics—it's a mature industry.

So what do you sell? I asked.

"Our ability to solve clients' problems"—what almost everyone sells today.

"Actually," he said, "my clients buy a relationship. With me."

We all sell intangibles—often in the form of "solutions"—and relationships.

Consider software makers. Software manufacturers once packaged their cheap-looking black discs into large colorful boxes. Why? Because the manufacturers had to make the discs look bigger and more valuable to justify the price.

As software matured and became more alike, its manufacturers began adding services to distinguish their software, calling it "value-added."

Today, what do software manufacturers sell? They offer software as a subscription service or as a give-away—typified by AOL's massive mailings of free discs. They no longer sell discs—products; they sell a growing array of services that pit software manufacturers not against other product manufacturers, but against Accenture and other firms—other *services*.

Consider the clever men behind TiVo. They seem to have created a device similar to a VCR. But what does their business plan say they are selling? Subscriptions to the services that come with their device.

As evidence of the ascendance of services, Hewlett-Packard recently bid to buy PricewaterhouseCoopers's consulting group, and Hitachi purchased Grant Thornton LLP's e-business consulting division. Traditional product manufacturers are becoming service providers with product manufacturing divisions.

TiVo, like almost everyone today, sells services.

Look at "value-added retailers." What is their value added? *Services.* Clients want VARs to sort through the jumble and recommend a reliable system. They want insight, advice, and support. They want—as that catch phrase of the past twenty-five years reminds us—a *solution.* If a solution happens to come with some products, fine.

People have become services, too. Our parents were employees. They joined companies where they expected to work for years and eventually "earn their gold watch."

Today, we change careers seven times in our lifetime. Business magazines tell us that we are Brands of One, Free Agents, and the Service Called You. At first those headlines sound ludicrous.

And then they don't.

We no longer are employees; we are services. In many industries, we are the Temp Agency of One. Twenty-five years ago a major issue in evaluating a job offer was the value of the employee benefits. Today, it is the portability of those benefits; can we move them easily to our next job?

But if virtually everyone and everything is a service, what do we *show* our prospects to sell our services and ourselves? If we were selling leather bags, you could let our prospects "see for themselves." Attractive? Obviously. Sturdy? It feels indestructible. Genuine? Smells like a handmade saddle.

But what if we are selling what we will do—our services? Our prospects cannot see them, and seeing is believing, which leads to buying.

How do we make our excellence visible?

That's our first challenge. Our next challenge is to establish trust, and our key weapon is a brand. People trust that brands will perform. More remarkably, however, is their second key impact. As examples like the tests for Extra Strength Rogaine show, brands make people believe that our branded products and services actually do perform well, *even when they do not.*

Brands create satisfaction.

In Rogaine's premarket

The growing belief that Google has become the world's cleanest, fastest, and best search engine was supported by the Wall Street Journal's well-regarded technology columnist, Walter Mossberg, in his March 1, 2000, column. Mossberg called Google "a beacon in a sea of confusion," "wicked fast," "thorough, speedy, smart and honest," and "simply the best search site I've ever used." Yet Yahoo! still was beating Google in the battle for users. Finally, Yahoo! conceded Google's superiority and bought the rights to use Google as its search engine.

tests, 40 percent of men who used Rogaine insisted that it grew hair—even though their "Rogaine" was just oil and water; they were in the control group in these tests. *Thinking they were using Rogaine made them see new hair.*

For years, the Internet portal and search engine Yahoo! cast the same spell. Most people thought Yahoo! was fun because it sounds fun. They also assumed because they saw the Yahoo! name so often, that it must be good; it appeared that everyone is using it. So they used Yahoo! and avoided demonstrably superior search engines like Google.

In this age of intangibles, this first principle: *Make your business and your excellence tangible and visible.* Those visible representations—your brand and its components, including your name, packaging, and price—attract clients and increase their satisfaction.

Georges Always Beat Als

We wanted to tell everyone who would win the 2000 election six months before voting day, but could not believe our data.

Every poll said our projected winner had no hope. Millions of Americans said George W. Bush didn't seem smart; Will Ferrell on *Saturday Night Live* became famous making jokes about it. George W. Bush seemed doomed by every account—but one.

In 1998 we had tested a theory about the influence of names by polling our name-testing panel, a group we use to discover the possible interpretations of proposed product and service names. We wanted to see if candidates' names influence elections.

We created a list of eighty-five men's first names—names we appeared to have chosen randomly. We asked the sixteen people to score each name for its strength and authoritativeness, then compared their scores for the first names of the candidates in every twentieth-century American presidential election. (Yes, Adlai and Calvin were among our eighty-five "random" names.)

The "stronger, more authoritative" name won every election.

As the 2000 election neared, I recalled that research, particularly "George's" high scores and "Al's" lower ones—a gap that suggested Bush would beat Gore.

And he did.

This test is not conclusive, but it certainly suggests what marketers often see: Names change how prospects and clients feel, and the buying decision they make.

Sweat your name.

What's in a Name?

On Friday, April 13, 2001, the online publishing company internet.com announced it was changing its name, to better reflect its activity in more conventional publishing—and to avoid the stigma that people attached to dot-coms.

On Monday, the markets opened. By day's end the company's stock was up 18 percent.

Names are golden.

The Familiarity Principle

You buy a new CD by a favorite group. You bring it home, play it, and feel disappointed: one good song on the whole disc.

You play it again. Hey, that other song sounds good, too. And you love the first one. As time goes by the number grows. After six listenings, the CD may become your favorite. What has happened?

Familiarity breeds attraction. The more you hear something, the more you like it.

The more you see someone, the more you tend to like them. R. F. Bornstein and two other psychologists demonstrated this in a 1987 experiment. The researchers subliminally flashed onto screens photos of the faces of several people—so quickly, in fact, that when interviewed later and shown the photos again, none of the subjects could recall ever seeing any of the faces before. Yet the more the person's face was flashed on the screen, the more the subjects liked that person when they met later.

Familiarity breeds liking.[*]

Consider another example. Anyone anywhere can buy stock in one of the seven Baby Bells, the regional phone companies created by the breakup of AT&T. In choosing one of those seven stocks, a prospect could read volumes on each Baby Bell, from earnings per share to decades' worth of press releases and news stories.

With all this information available, and with their presumed desire to invest in the most promising Baby Bell, what do investors do?

They pick the Baby Bell in their region.

These investors have no inside information. Denver investors know no more about their local Baby Bell, Qwest, than Qwest investors in Dubrovnik.

These investors are not relying on information. *They are buying based on familiarity.* The Denver investor sees Qwest's name on billboards, signs, trucks—a dozen places. When she decides to invest, she buys Qwest not because its future looks better, but because it's familiar. She feels she knows Qwest, though she knows little about it. Her knowledge comforts her.

[*]This research was reported in R. F. Bornstein, D. R. Leone, and D. J. Galley, "The Generalizability of Subliminal Mere Exposure Effects," *Journal of Personality and Social Psychology* 53 (1987): 1070–79, and referred to in *Influence: The Psychology Persuasion,* Robert B. Cialdini, New York: Quill (1993).

What is familiarity worth? Consider Corporate Branding LLC's study of the stock performance of the thirty-two companies with the most familiar and favorably viewed brands.

> *"Nothing except the mint can make money without advertising."*
>
> —*Thomas Macaulay*

In that decade, the thirty companies that made up the Dow Jones Industrial Average generated a 309 percent average return on investment, and the 500 Standard & Poor's 500 companies returned 308 percent. And the thirty-two companies with the most familiar brands?

402 percent.

Brands build familiarity—and business.

Get known.

To Know You Is to Love You

Everyone knows the phrase "familiarity breeds contempt." In business, it builds esteem.

As evidence, look at the remarkably close relationship between "share of mind" and "esteem" for these well-known companies, as measured by Landor Associates:

Levi's: 58 percent/63 percent
General Motors: 65 percent/60 percent
Pepsi: 67 percent/61 percent

You find similar correlations in much smaller companies, for a reason you can find among your experiences. You face two choices for dry cleaning, for example: a cleaners you've heard of and one you haven't.

"I've heard of them, they must be okay," your inner voice advises. You choose the one you know, and worry about the one you don't.

Get known. Choose a memorable name and display it so prominently—such as on your briefcase and luggage tags—that people can read it ten feet away.

To know you is to prefer you.

Make your name known fast.

What Fidelity and Vanguard Show You

In 1999, Janus, Fidelity, and Vanguard represented three of the Big Five American mutual funds.

In a survey of U.S. households, Americans ranked these three companies first, second, and third for performance.

Only Janus, however, was what it appeared to be. Its family of funds ranked first of the leading fifty-four fund families. Fidelity and Vanguard, however, lagged many percentage points behind—in 35th and 37th place respectively.

Meanwhile, a tiny fund family named BlackRock rocked in 1999, ranking 8th in performance. But its net sales totaled just $5 million—compared to $36 *billion* for Janus and $14 *billion* each for Fidelity and Vanguard. BlackRock won big, yet lost.

If prospects have heard of you, you must be good. If they have heard a lot about you, you must be great—even if you aren't.

Remember BlackRock: Familiarity beats performance.

Familiarity and the New 80/20 Rule

The Big Five—Janus, Fidelity, Vanguard, Pimco, and Alliance—currently comprise about 1 percent of America's fund families, yet are capturing 85 percent of the net cash flow into U.S. funds.

Business books frequently mention the 80/20 Rule, which holds that 20 percent of your efforts will produce 80 percent of your rewards, 20 percent of salespeople make 80 percent of all sales, and, in the fish story variation, that 20 percent of fishermen catch 80 percent of the fish.

But these Big Five companies hold almost 500

times more in total assets than the average competitive fund—suggesting that the impact of a brand may be the dramatic and explosive exception to the 80/20 rule.

Brands don't help companies edge their competitors; they help them crush them.

Remember the 85/1 Rule: Brands crush their competition.

Understanding Your Brand: Gerber Unbaby Food and Salty Lemonade

Gerber tried to market adult food, and failed.

Frito-Lay tried lemonade, and failed.

American Express is trying to sell discount brokerage, and it's failing.

All three companies ran into obstacles you might hit, too: their brands.

Gerber is baby food. Adult baby food sounds awful.

Frito-Lay is salty snacks. Salty lemonade sounds disgusting.

American Express is a prestige club. A prestigious discount brokerage sounds like an oxymoron.

None of these companies could leap outside their brand, and neither can you—or Empower.

Empower is the alias for a successful regional staffing company. In 1998 Empower's executives, like many American executives, realized that consulting was irresistibly profitable. They could not ignore Exhibit A for this proposition, Arthur Andersen. Andersen had mutated from a successful CPA firm into a much more profitable accounting and consulting firm, before imploding into two separate firms—primarily because the consultants became tired of sharing their greater wealth with Andersen's accountants. (A smart and, as history turned out, lucky move.)

Hundreds of American businesses mimicked Arthur Andersen and added consulting to their services. By 1999 even Microsoft was calling itself a consultancy, focused on information technology, systems integration, and Internet and intranet implementation.

Empower's executives saw a major opportunity in its clients' needs for advice on human-resources-related issues such as recruitment, staffing, hiring, and training. But these executives' question should not have been, Did Empower's clients need that advice? Of course they did, just as people want "adult food," lemonade, and discount brokerage. Empower needed to ask, Would Empower's clients buy those services from Empower? Would companies buy human resources consulting from a staffing company?

Most would not. The reason was not that Empower lacked the talent, experience, or skills.

Empower lacked the brand.

Staffing companies have a brand reputation: They are Organizers. The good ones can assure you that next Monday, sixty able people will arrive at your doors to do defined jobs for a limited time. Staffing companies are not Thinker-Solvers—the well-educated and well-versed individuals who can see big

pictures and solve one big problem. Staffing companies see small pictures and solve dozens of smaller
problems.

Organizers are not Thinker-Solvers. That means
that staffing companies cannot be consulting firms—
just like Fritos cannot make lemonade.

Empower tried to reach beyond the limits of its
brand, and like Gerber, Frito-Lay, American Express,
and others, it was bound to fail.

Your brand has limits, too.

If you want to offer services outside your brand, establish a separate and separately named unit, or fund
a new operation off-site. (Even putting two businesses under one roof can dilute each brand.)

As an alternative, ally with a company with an en-
trée into your market. (Empower, for example, could
have aligned with a consultancy that lacked human
resources consulting.) Offer that ally shared engage-
ments, contacts with your key clients, and other in-
centives.

Whatever you do, recognize that part of a brand's
power comes from its intense concentration in a narrow but rich market. Lose that concentration by trying
to expand your brand and you might lose your
brand—and all its rewards.

Look before you leap outside your brand.

The Limits of Every Brand

Imagine you are producing a documentary on D-Day.

You place in *Variety* a help-wanted ad seeking a writer for your film.

The day after your ad appears, you receive two responses, each with a cover letter and a résumé from a writer.

The first résumé: award-winning writer of brochures, advertisements, press releases, industrial and commercial films, documentaries, advertisements, and feature articles.

The second: experienced documentary writer/ producer specializing in modern American and European military history.

Who do you hire?

Question two, perhaps as important: If you needed a press release for your D-Day documentary, would you hire the first candidate? Or would you wait for a better candidate?

You'd wait. Even if your first candidate could write brilliant press releases, you'd assume he couldn't. He was stretched too thin, doing too much. We always think specialists are better than generalists. A Jack-of-All-Trades is the Master of None.

People once believed in the Generalist. People living in 1560, for example, believed that Erasmus knew everything. In 1500, a person *could* know everything; he could read every book in the world's largest library by reading a book a week for four years. People do not believe, for example, that the same person can write dozens of hit songs, host *The Tonight Show,* act in both dramas and comedies, write uproarious comedy, play the piano, and produce articulate essays on ethics.

In short, we no longer believe that Steve Allen could exist.

The Information Age and the ever-increasing complexity of life, however, killed the Renaissance man, the Steve Allen, the Master-of-Many-Trades. People today believe that no person or firm can excel at many tasks, and that only specialists can excel at any one.

To be seen as excellent, a quality every client seeks, you must narrow your specialty.

Know your limits—especially the one that your brand imposes.

A Thousand Words?

In the 1980s, a revealing quiz circulated through America's businesses. It asked people to study dozens of symbols of famous companies and match the company to the symbol.

Few people could identify even 25 percent of the symbols. Few people, in fact, could match one. The symbols, which were various forms of squares, circles, and triangles meant to look sophisticated and contemporary, looked meaningless and indistinguishable.

To further embarrass the companies and designers behind the symbols, the quiz's author included excerpts from several companies' press releases. A typical release announced that Heroic International's new triangle symbol suggested energy and dynamism. Because the triangle is the Greek letter delta, the symbol of change in the sciences, the triangle communicates change to people, even those without calculus and physics backgrounds.

What did people see in these triangles? They saw musical triangles, yield signs, or pyramids with lines on them. Others saw Egypt, mountain peaks, and dunce caps. No one—no one—saw *change*.

In creating your symbols—words or pictures—you must recognize the first law of communicating: It is not what you say; it is what people hear. It is not what you communicate; it is what gets communicated.

If you need to explain your symbol, it isn't communicating.

Your symbols must convey your quality and uniqueness. If you wish to be considered innovative, you cannot use a symbol used by other innovative companies. If people think you are just another small company, your symbols—words and images—must attack that perception immediately.

But whatever you say, say *something*. Get the word out; get some word out. Because more messages are inundating people with less time to process them, your symbols that communicate the most will sell the most.

Communicate volumes. Use pictures.

Understanding Symbols

"Don't give me some symbol for our company," the executive of the professional service insists. "We aren't like a soft drink. We have a story. Let's just tell it."

The executive misunderstands. You tell your story with words, perhaps, but words are only symbols, too. When you say "blue," your word "blue" is not the color. The word merely symbolizes the color. When you write "blue," that written word is not the color, it is only a written symbol for the spoken word.

Written words, in other words, are just symbols of symbols.

Just as important, many images are more vivid than words. You react far more strongly to seeing an American flag than you do to reading the following two words, "American flag." The Nazi flag provokes more outrage than the word "Nazi," just as the flag of the Confederacy continues to provoke more controversy than the word "Dixie." And we can safely assume that far fewer Dixie cups would be sold if they were emblazoned with even a tiny Confederate flag.

Images are more real than words.

You must tell your stories with "mere symbols"; you have no other way. And because visual symbols are more vivid and real, visual images are the simplest, fastest, and most memorable way to communicate.

A symbol can speak a thousand words. In today's overcommunicated era, that is more than your words ever will convey.

In today's world, symbols speak louder than words.

Understanding Symbols: The 1965 Pirates

The 1964 Neah-Kah-Nie Pirates football team had performed pitifully. Previewing the Pirates' final game against the also winless Banks Braves, the Portland *Oregonian* dubbed the contest the Futility Bowl (Neah-Kah-Nie won by the almost predictable bad game score: 7–0).

Just nine months later, most of the Pirates' players returned for the 1965 season.

Little about the 1965 Neah-Kah-Nie Pirates had changed from the previous year. A fan might notice two minor changes, however, one on each side of each helmet. Above the helmet's right ear hole were red stars the size of quarters, each symbolizing an outstanding defensive play by that player.

Over the other ear, a more vivid symbol: the pirate skull and crossbones.

The Pirates took the field that September. By year's end the team set school records for defense—fumbles caused and recovered and interceptions—and allowed fewer than two touchdowns a game. Just a year after the 1-8, Futility Bowl season, the Pirates won seven games and lost just two.

From 1-8 to 7-2, from the *Oregonian*'s Futility Bowl to its number-eleven-ranked team in the state—was it the players? They were just the 1964 sophomores and juniors one year later. Something clearly had changed, however.

It was the symbols. The Pirates played like Pirates because they looked like them. They hit harder because the symbols communicated, "You are a Pirate. Play like one." The red stars acted like battle ribbons and inspired the players to earn them.

Symbols and images change attitudes. Researchers in the late 1990s found, for example, that people really do think bad guys wear black. Professional football referees penalized teams clad in black more often than any others—and more often than they penalized that same team when it wore lighter colors.

The Union Jack, the Confederate flag, camouflage clothing, "the finger"—symbols inspire and calm, provoke and evoke. As simple as they are—and in large part, *because* they are as simple as they are in our complicated ages—symbols work. They can encourage, inspire, and change the people who use them.

Like those 1965 Pirates.

Symbols talk and symbols touch.

Lessons from Lowe's

Lowe's stores are working, but their name isn't.

Thirty years ago, the name Lowe's for a chain of home stores would have worked. Names mattered less when there were fewer companies and less competition. If you own your town's only home store, you can call it Petunia, Peter, or Penelope. It barely matters. You are *the* home store.

Even when some competition entered, the name still wasn't critical. Prospects could get a Phillips screwdriver at Acme or Superior. With fewer choices, prospects could learn enough about each choice to distinguish them.

Today choices have multiplied and remultiplied. Prospects now can now choose from seven Premiers, five Superiors, and dozens of others. They can't keep their choices straight.

Today, Lowe's has a problem with investors. With such a proliferation of names, investors hear Lowe's and think of Loew's, the movie theaters, at a time when theaters including Loew's are closing everywhere, the result of an orgy of overbuilding in the 1990s.

> *Because our brains take things that appear similar and file them together, we readily confuse products and services with similar names. Casual fans of art regularly confuse Monet and Manet, for example. Students of literature hear the title "Ode to a Grecian Urn" and immediately know that Yeats or Keats wrote it—but which one, they wonder.*

For years, advertising agency prospects confused Benton & Bowles with BBDO, just as more recent prospects phone MartinWilliams after seeing work by The Martin Agency that they admire.

What's in a name? Too often, confusion.

In the Era of Mass Choice, how do you increase your chances of being chosen? You must distinguish yourself immediately—in your name.

Don't confuse people. Choose an unconfusable name.

Move Your Message Up

You run an executive recruitment and staffing firm that works with corporate clients in just five industries. (Good strategy: People prefer specialists to generalists.) Although most staffing firms are small and local, yours often handles assignments outside North America.

Given your two important distinctions—your five-industry specialization and your international experience—you must avoid the typical generic name that characterizes your industry (names like FirstStaff, ExecSearch, ProStaff, and their many clones). Instead, you must convey "specialized and international" in your name.

Consider, for example, using a non-English, and therefore international-sounding, word for *specialized*. Italian offers you one: *specialiste*.

Then, to remove any ambiguity, add a descriptor to your new company name. On your business cards, signs, brochures, and ads, your company signature could now read:

"Specialiste. Specialized international staffing."

From this new name alone, most prospects will assume you are more experienced and skilled than the typical regional firm. By conspicuously listing the five industries in which you specialize, your prospects will see that you specialize in their industry, which is always a desirable trait.

(A first principle of business and marketing: Everyone believes that their industry is unique. You must approach every client with this in mind.)

Your new name conveys and constantly reminds people what makes you distinctive and good. Consider these good names (though not necessarily good businesses):

Stamps.com. Obviously, it's a place—quite possibly *the* place—to buy stamps online.

LivePerson. Great: It's a service that gives your Web site a human voice, somehow. Better look into it.

SmartForce. Electronic employee training, especially for salespeople.

These names quickly convey the distinctions of their respective services. They get the company's message into its name.

Getting your message into your name will improve your marketing and simplify your selling. In this age of a million choices, a name that conveys your distinction immediately will get on more short lists and into more presentations. Even better, people will remember your distinction and recognize that you have one, and always see one good reason to choose you.

Move your message up.

Kinko's Cleverness

You want some good Italian food. Which restaurant would you choose: "Italian Cuisine" or "Giuseppi's"?

Giuseppi's. You associate generic or ordinary names like Italian Cuisine with mundane services.

That association seems obvious. Then why do millions of firms choose dull names like Fast Printing, Consulting Associates, or most remarkably of all, "Law Offices"?

Kinko's did not crush its fast printing competitors just with superior service. It pulverized them with a name everyone remembers—a unique name that sounds countercultural and makes prospects assume that Kinko's is unique.

Oregon's northern coast is the home of the world's most generically named business. Above this gift shop in tiny Garibaldi, pop. 375, is a sign with the name "Stuff and Things."

Kinko's name does not name the enterprise. *The name burns itself into people's minds.* They hear the name once and remember it a week later, while Kinko's competitors must repeat their names dozens of times to be remembered.

Kinko's name also suggests an attitude—a time when people might reexperience the freer years they loved. Kinko's competitors' names like Copies to Go, by contrast, promise their clients that they will experience nothing. Its name alone gives Kinko's a competitive edge.

Kinko's name begins the marketing of its stores. It sets the stores apart, gives prospects a positive feeling, and delivers messages that reduce the burden on its salespeople and marketing communications.

To seem special, sound it.

Why Copy Shops Struggle

A corporate trainer stops at Rapit Printing in downtown Pittsburgh and makes twelve copies of an upcoming presentation.

A month later, on the night before her presentation, she discovers she needs forty more copies. She remembers those twelve copies she made at, she recalls—"Insty Prints." She calls Insty Prints to confirm they are open, then she gets in her car and retraces her route of a month before, to Rapit Printing. It's closed.

InstyPrints, RapitPrinting, SpeedyPrint—who knows, what's the difference, who can tell them apart?

This story is happening right now; people are confusing companies with similar names. They are urging friends whose firms need technology consulting to call IMI, when they meant EDS. They are driving their bashed-in Saturn to the Collision Center on their friends' recommendations of Collision Company.

And they are driving to Rapit Printing thinking it's Insty Prints.

Pepsi knows this problem well. Huge percentages of people who see Pepsi commercials think they are advertising Coke. The reverse happens, too, but less often.

When you choose a common and therefore easily confused name for your company, you advertise your competitors and squander another opportunity to make your name known.

Avoid a common name.

Sir Isaac Newton, Human Being

Odd, that headline.

Newton obviously was human. Why those unnecessary words?

Newton doesn't need them, just as eBay doesn't need to add to its name "online auction services." It's just eBay. Just as it's just Amazon, Fallon, and Russell Reynolds. Those Young Turks on Sandhill Road may legally be registered as "Benchmark Venture Capital," but everyone knows them only as Benchmark.

Your name should name you, not describe you. If you add extra description, everyone will remove it—just as they've chopped *Bank* from Wells Fargo, *Television* from CNN, and *Restaurant* from Patina and Charlie Trotter's.

Name your business, then stop. Any added information will slow your communication, shrink the conspicuousness of your logo, and keep people from remembering your name.

It's a name, not a description.

Omaha Surfing and Jefferson Airplane

Paul Alexander called his 1991 biography of Sylvia Plath *Rough Magic*. The title stopped browsers in their path through bookstores. How can magic be rough? customers wondered, and bought the book to answer the question.

What if *Selling the Invisible* had been titled *Marketing Services Today*? It would be sitting on markdown tables, begging for customers' money. But "Selling the Invisible"? How can you sell what no one can see? people wondered—and bought the book to find the answer.

Contradictions captivate. People feel compelled to unravel these puzzles, get closure, and remove the discomfort of uncertainty.

Consider the beer Irish Red. This contradiction works subtly, but well. People associate Ireland with green. Red is green's opposite—directly opposite, in fact, on a color wheel. The contradiction between Ireland and Red takes hold. We remember Irish Red.

Alpine Climbing School features a sixty-five-foot artificial rock used for practice climbing. The ho-hum name, however, makes the school sound ordinary, and fails to suggest its distinctive feature: that mammoth rock.

To convey that distinction, the school should consider a contradictory name—like Little Everest. That name would also make the school sound fun to novices and less experienced climbers, a large group the school must reach to grow.

Think of contradictions you have encountered. They stopped and seized you, and never left you.

Jefferson Airplane, for example. There's a Jefferson Monument and Memorial—but a Jefferson Airplane? That name was even more provocative in its time, because rock bands' names prior to Buffalo Springfield and Jefferson Airplane always

> *In 2001, the marketers advertising the book* Amanda's Wedding *clearly understood the stopping power of contradictions. Their headline read:*
> *"You are cordially invited to a fiasco."*

used the plural, like Beatles, Supremes, and Crickets. A singular name for a group of people was a startling—and therefore effective—contradiction.

War and Peace? Simultaneously? Shouldn't it read War, *then* Peace? But what if Tolstoy had given his classic that more conventional, uncontradictory name?

Contradictions are odd, and oddness works. Odd names imprint on memories—including your prospects'.

To find a memorable name, try contradicting yourself.

Clients Love Odd Things

Tropical North is a good name for a tanning salon in Frostbite Falls, but more prospects notice and remember Red Hot Tundra.

Why?

After all, each name conveys the same idea. At four syllables each and thirteen and twelve letters respectively, neither name is too long.

Red Hot Tundra works better, partly because Americans rarely use the word "tundra," yet have vague enough recollections of geography classes to sense the contradiction between "tundra," which is found in arctic climates, and "red hot."

In addition, "red hot" beats "tropical." That adjective has a visual element—redness—and a tactile element—hot to the touch—tropical lacks. The more senses that a word appeals to, the more easily people remember it.

Find an uncommon name. Uncommon names stand out from the noise and will make your name familiar to people, sooner.

Unusual names get you noticed and remembered.

Blue Martini, Loudcloud, and Other Odd Ducks

While few words retain much value in commerce, not all is lost.

Blue Martini roared into its IPO in the summer of 2000 and roared out with a valuation of $12 a share, another coup for President Monte Zweben.

Marc Andreessen, the founder of Netscape, got the attention of millions when he announced as his second act Loudcloud.

Yahoo! continues to confound the experts with its domination of the Internet portal and search engine business and high market valuation.

Like several older companies, these companies discovered the power of the unusual—of companies called Blue Martini, Loudcloud, and Yahoo!

Federal Express realized this power with "When it absolutely positively has to be there overnight." A redundancy like "absolutely positively" in a slogan, which by definition is succinct, was unheard of. That unusual element made the theme stick—and helped the service fly.

The founders of Toys "Я" Us recognized this power when it chose that deliberately odd name, executed in a deliberately odd way. A backward letter? What was that?

Oddness works.

If everyone feels comfortable with your proposed

name, it's probably too familiar, and probably won't work. Keep searching.

Make yourself uncomfortable.

How to Think Odd

Over two hundred Minneapolis–St. Paul firms are named "Summit," "Pinnacle," or "Alpine." (I cannot guess and probably cannot count the number of firms in Denver, an area that actually has mountains, that use one of these three names.)

None of these two hundred companies enjoys conspicuous success, and each is handicapped. Their names will not brand where names must: in the minds of people.

If these firms insist on being associated with peaks, they should consider the name 26,000 Feet instead, or, to evoke smiles from pop music fans, Eight Miles High.

If you insist on using familiar metaphors to name your firm, find an unfamiliar way to express it. In the case of Alpine, take that mountain metaphor and stretch it—as the inventors of an exceptional search engine did. After spending several days staring at possible names on their erasable boards in their Palo Alto offices, someone accidentally found an unusual alternative.

Why not the name Alta Vista—Latin for "view from a high point"? A common metaphor now becomes more memorable, and demonstrates a key principle in naming: look beyond the obvious.

In naming, never stop at the first word or phrase that conveys your message. Your first associations are too commonplace. Go deeper into your memories, experiences, and associations.

What do you associate with mountains? Is *Base Camp* a better name than *Summit*? What about *Timberline*, *Crampon*, *Himalaya*, or *Sherpa*?

Keep going beyond your first free associations. If you are opening a Greek catering service, don't stop with *Athens, Parthenon,* or *Greek Islands*. Build associations off each of those words. Your new list now will include *Zorba, Corinth, Mykonos, Delphi, Plato, Aristotle, Socrates, Peloponnese*. Eventually at least one strong name will pop out—one that implies more than just Greece, but other qualities you wish to convey, like wisdom, friendliness, or celebration, for example.

The Alta Vista name arose by accident. Someone had written "Palo Alto" and "Vista" on a white board. Then someone erased "Palo." "Alto Vista, hey, that could be a good name?" a third person offered. A fourth then put the name in proper Latin, "Alta Vista."

While more memorable than names like Summit, the Alta Vista name suffers from being too esoteric for its market. Not surprisingly, Alta Vista leads Yahoo! in only one market segment: research librarians, who are well educated and erudite, and more likely to understand what the words Alta Vista mean.

The most memorable names are out there—but you must keep climbing to reach them.

To find an uncommon name, take your first set of names, and free-associate.

Hit Your Prospects in the Nose, Too

An entrepreneur recently opened a creative think tank and felt thrilled with its name: *Velocity*. But while that name is short and not overused, it accomplishes little, partly because it does not imprint well. We do not remember "Velocity."

Why?

Because the word "velocity" has no smell, sound, taste, feel, or image. You cannot *sense* velocity. That word conveys little more than its more common synonym, "speed."

"Whoosh!" works better. Its distinctive, slightly funny, windy sound rushes through your brain like the wind; you hear it.

Whoosh is *sensory*.

Red Hot Chili Peppers. Many people who never heard the group's music remember that name, because they can see and taste a red pepper. *Red Hot Chili Peppers* is sensory.

The more sensory your name, the more it will imprint and register, and the more familiar it will become.

Appeal to people's senses—as many as possible.

A Powerful Tool for Branding

How can you be sure that people will respond to your name—even love it?

Have an independent party test your proposed name on a dozen verbal and intelligent people. (Lawyers, journalists, and other people from verbal, information-dominated businesses are especially adept at seeing the implications of words.)

Listen to their responses. You often will be surprised. (Most women, for example, do not like transparently feminine names for services.)

Listen carefully and use that information to guide your choice.

To discover a name that people will love, ask twelve.

Finding Your Perfect Name: The Descriptive Name

The English language may seem infinite—the existence of twenty-six definitions in my dictionary for the word "read" suggests this problem—but we are lucky. In naming a company, our options shrink to a manageable number: six.

Once you understand these six options you can ignore more than half the routes that most people follow in search of names. With rare exceptions, only two routes work.

Let's begin with the routes that do not. First, you might try a descriptive name. It's the name that merely describes what your company does, such as QuickPrint, Computer Consultants, or Children's Clinic.

Descriptive names are ordinary and difficult to remember. They work logically but fail emotionally; they evoke no feelings. Descriptive names also tend to suggest an ordinary, nonprofessional service, because skilled professional services rarely use them.

As a test, what is your impression of a company named "Small Business Public Accounts"? Do they sound skilled and professional?

Not likely.

Beware of descriptive names.

The Perfect Name, Option Two: An Acronym

ACP, APB, ABC, AEC, AIM, AMA, ADP.

How are you doing remembering all of those?

Not well?

With rare exceptions—such as the American Conservatory Theater, known as ACT—people cannot remember acronyms, and confuse them with other acronyms. (Talking to the CFO of a major ad agency, I mentioned my client ADP, the Fortune 500 provider of payroll and other services to businesses. She said she knew the company. "They handle our building security," she said. ADT actually provided that service.)

Acronyms express or imply nothing, rational or emotional, and are forgotten as quickly as they are said.

Monogram your shorts, not your signs.

Option Three: The Neologism

Sentra, Compaq, Reliastar, Accenture. What are those, anyway?

Those names are neologisms—new words made

from existing prefixes and suffixes. The names for the Sentra car (from the word "sentry," meant to connote safety) and the health care company Humana are neologisms. They also illustrate the problem with neologisms.

Neologisms tend to suggest something that is new and technological. This connotation makes many prospects uneasy; they prefer proven, reliable services. As evidence, consider your response to a group psychology practice called Serena. Despite the partners' well-meaning attempt to suggest peace of mind (serenity), that name sounds cool and detached.

Perhaps worst, most neologisms reveal the too heavy hands of the marketers behind them. They tend to sound contrived and manipulative—a huge mistake.

Considering a neologism? Reconsider.

Option Four: The Geographic Name

Omaha Surfing might be a good name for a surfboard shop. The name Boston Consulting works because it links the firm to a city associated with Harvard and other well-regarded colleges, which makes the name appealing to credential-oriented prospects looking for smart consultants.

Names for technology firms that communicate their

Silicon Valley locations also work; they suggest a company stocked with computer-heads. Silicon Valley Bank's name works, too, because it suggests, as it should, that the bank specializes in venture-financed start-ups. New York hotels with "Park" in their name convey the prestige and view of their locations on Central Park.

But these are among the relatively few exceptions to the rule: Geography-based names usually fail.

You should consider a geographic name if your location implies something positive and if you are willing to accept two other traits of geographic names: They usually do not resonate emotionally and, because they tend to be a common name, usually are forgettable.

You may find a good geographic name for your company—but it isn't likely.

A geographic name might work.

Option Five: The Personal Name (But of Course)

Your name could be *your* name—literally.

Personal names—such as Mayo Clinic, Covington & Burling, and Charles Schwab, which use the names of the firm's founders or principals—work well for many services. Because law, accounting, and executive search firms have used personal names almost exclusively and for centuries, a personal name connotes professionalism.

Personal names also create a unique, self-reinforcing benefit loop—a kind of marketing Möbius strip. When people whose names are included in the firm name get good publicity, the entire firm's reputation is enhanced. Its brand increases in value.

Similarly, if the firm gets favorable press, even for work in which the named partners were not involved, the named partners benefit. Their reputations improve.

For these reasons, firms in which key members are likely to publish or become public figures should strongly consider a name that includes its key members' names.

The reverse is true, too. If the proposed named partner tends to hide from public view, this self-reinforcing loop argument for a personal name disappears.

In considering a personal name, however, beware of three considerations.

First, as John DeLorean and Michael Milken remind us, reputations change. Make sure the pillars for your name are solid.

Your second risk involves the Smith and Jones Phenomenon. Many last names are common, which makes them easy to forget and easy to confuse with other firms using the same names.

Finally, person-based names easily can get too long, i.e., anything longer than four syllables. Windsor & Hill works; it is short enough to read conspicuously in an ad or on a luggage tag and to be processed and remembered. Willingham & Hill works less well, however, and Willingham & Hilliard fails.

Explore personal names. More than any other category of name, they naturally sound personal—a quality of a desirable service. Personal names also signal to your clients who is responsible. Clients of David Boies's law firm know they can call David. Clients of Consulting Partners, on the other hand, feel helpless.

Your best name may be your founder's.

Primrose and Yahoo!: The Evocative Name

Yahoo!

You know it's a better name for a search engine than Lycos, Northern Light, or that colossal error of a name, WebCrawler. Why?

Because its name resonates emotionally. It makes you smile. Because you've never heard a company name like it before, you remember Yahoo! because it's unusual. You remember Yahoo! but forget its competitors—and forget to use them for searches.

Primrose is an evocative name, used by Alzheimer's living centers in Santa Rosa, California. "Primrose" evokes the outdoors. This helps contrast Primrose, with its emphasis on outdoor activities and gardens, with similar facilities, many of which have a more indoor emphasis and institutional feeling. The embedded word "prim" in Primrose also subtly suggests the cleanliness and tidiness of these residences, another contrast to many similar facilities.

The names Yahoo! and Primrose *evoke*. They evoke

feelings—a signal and powerful trait of most evocative names.

Evocative words also have a nice inkblot quality; they usually inspire more than one positive interpretation. Primrose suggests outdoors, cleanliness, bright colors, healthfulness, and vitality—far more associations than you could create with a descriptive name such as Special Care Court, a personal name such as Shelby & Magers, or the firm's original name, Heritage Court.

Evocative names are not for everyone; traditional professional firms, such as lawyers and accountants, should think carefully before considering one. With those exceptions, however, evocative names touch people, take root in their minds, and warm your sales calls, often with curiosity and almost always with good feelings.

Look for an evocative name.

A Checklist for Avoiding the Lake Tahoe Name

The perfect company name pops into your head. Hallelujah!

Don't let that feeling fool you.

Venture-capitalized start-ups often invite me to Silicon Valley to help name their companies. We meet, then I board the last Northwest Airlines flight back to

Minneapolis (the 5:05), get seated, and start jotting down names.

Eureka! The perfect name comes to me, usually over Lake Tahoe. (This happens so often my partner V.C. has learned to call it "the Lake Tahoe Name.") I feel my heart thumping and my palms dampening. More than once, I've done some quick math that showed that I've just earned $65,000 per hour. What a business, I think. What a life.

What a mistake.

By the time the 737 gets over South Dakota, my get-rich-in-a-minute name has plummeted to earth, killed by some fatal flaw.

To avoid those flaws, check your proposed name against these tests. (Rules are for breaking, of course, but break these only with good reason.)

- Can your proposed name be pronounced easily, even musically?
- Can you say it without regularly being asked to spell it?
- Does it read quickly and clearly—or does the reader have to pause to consider it?
- Is it spelled as it sounds? (Jargon tip: Some professional "namists" refer to this as "phonetic transparency.") If not, can you easily explain how to spell it? (Example: "Especiale is special with an e added on both ends.")
- Is it short—eleven letters and four syllables maximum?
- Does it contain negative "internal words"? (Example: Accenture contains the internal word "cen-

sure," which has a negative meaning, connotation, and sound.)

- Is it unique and sensory, two traits that make words memorable?
- Is it interesting? Does it have "story value" or a "backstory"?
- Is it authentic? Is it who you really are?
- Can your employees say it proudly?
- Does it set the right tone?
- Is it different enough from your competitors' names? From noncompetitors' names?
- Is it acceptable to almost every important prospect?
- Do a few people dislike it? (A good sign. Good names have edges.)
- Does it make people uneasy? (An even better sign. A candidate for a top position at Yahoo! said she'd take the job if the company dropped its name. A more flexible candidate said he'd accept a top position if Yahoo! dropped their exclamation point.)
- Does it express or imply a desirable message?
- Is it *meaning-rich:* Does it imply more than one positive message? (Some good names do not meet this test, but many great names do.)

Before you pick your name, test it.

Harley, Ogilvy, and the Incredible Shrinking Names

Remember Federal Express?

On June 22, 1994, a Federal Express airplane landed in Memphis and was rushed to a nearby hangar. Twenty minutes later, the plane came back out. It had changed identity. On its side was the new word:

"FedEx."

A student of names could have predicted this. The human brain rejects names of more than four syllables, and abbreviates them. The brain turned Harley-Davidson into Harley, and Ogilvy & Mather into Ogilvy. Law firm partners have learned that unless their name is first or second on the letterhead, no one will use it.

Federal Express had learned that, too, and also had learned that its name didn't play well everywhere. Many movie fans and Latin American history buffs know why: In Latin American countries, *federales* are the bad guys.

The tendency of Americans to speed up everything seems to be growing. Representatives of Lowry Hill, the wealth management firm, began noticing in 2001 that many of their clients and friends were simply calling the firm "Lowry."

Federal Express's new, shorter name solved several problems but produced an added benefit. To fit the old name on its most powerful advertising medium—the sides of its trailers—Federal Express could not use letters taller than four feet, ten inches.

By shrinking its name from fourteen characters to five, however, the firm now could print much more visible letters—six feet tall. Now the new company name could be displayed more conspicuously—as you learned when you first spotted a FedEx plane hundreds of yards away.

Companies learn another value of brief names when they advertise. To fit into all but the largest print ads, long names must be printed in relatively small type. Shorter names can be printed in far more conspicuous type and ensure the ad does what today's marketing communications must: make their name more familiar.

Small names act bigger.

Churchill Was Right: Your Package Is Your Service

Every service ultimately sells an experience: the experience of receiving the service. But what is that experience?

We assume that service providers provide that experience by the way they serve their customers; we assume that customer service *is* the experience. We are half right.

The practical Winston Churchill hinted at the missing half when he observed, "People shape buildings, then buildings shape people."

Your environment—your building, setting, the entire surroundings of your client's experience—does not merely package you. It changes, and becomes a critical part of, each client's experience.

Great "packages":

- Restrooms at the Felix restaurant, Hong Kong
- Cirque du Soleil stage, Bellagio Hotel, Las Vegas
- ESales brochures, Morningstar
- MyExcite customized home page, Excite.com
- Web site, Winespectator.com
- Rooms, the Shutters Hotel, Santa Monica, California
- Brasserie (restaurant), Seagram Building, New York City
- Institute of Contemporary Art, Boston, Massachusetts
- Jake's Famous Crawfish and Mother's Bistro, restaurants, Portland, Oregon
- Costumes and set design, The Lion King
- Newer athletic facilities (excludes current football stadium), Stanford University, Palo Alto, California
- Priority letters, FedEx
- Asia de Cuba (restaurant), New York City
- Camden Yards baseball park, Baltimore
- Sephora department store, Champs-Elysées, Paris
- The Microsoft Museum, Bellevue, Washington
- The Smithsonian Air & Space Museum, Washington, D.C.
- The Quadrangle, University of Virginia, Charlottesville, Virginia
- Headquarters, TBWA Chiat\Day (advertising), Venice, California

The evidence for this surrounds us. Place violent children in a pink room and what happens? The California children's probation department found that pink rooms calm children. They have fewer outbursts.

Paint a bridge blue and what happens? Some Londoners learned when they painted Blackfriar's Bridge blue, hoping it would discourage suicides. It did.

Paint a ceiling blue and what happens? The people under it become smarter. People in blue-ceilinged rooms score up to 12 percent higher in IQ tests than people in control groups.

Your environment is your client's experience. Your environment changes and complements the experience, changes perceptions, and alters your client's moods—and perhaps, it appears, even their intelligence.

The environment is the experience. Make yours exceptional.

Imagineering's Six Commandments

Few lessons from Disney's success can help you more than "Mickey's Commandments." Laid down by Marty Sklar, president of Disney's Imagineering Division, the commandments are intended to guide building and space designers, but apply to everything from your lobbies to your letterheads:

1. Wear your guest's shoes; don't forget the human factor.
2. Create a "wienie" (a visual centerpiece that draws people to it).
3. Avoid overload.
4. Tell one story at a time.
5. Avoid visual contradictions; maintain a consistent identity.
6. Keep it up. (Even the slightest thing out of order will diminish a client's expectations.)

Follow the Commandments.

Clients Understand with Their Eyes

To see how we process information, consider this typical conversation:

"Do you *see* what I'm saying?

"Not really."

"Look, *picture* this. You're holding a bird. Should you let loose of the bird in your hand for the chance to grab two birds you see in a bush?"

"Oh, I *see*."

These verbs reveal how people develop an understanding of ideas. We picture them. Visual images develop like Polaroids in "our mind's eye"—another revealing expression.

To be heard and understood, your message must be seen.

Until your prospects have a picture, your business is merely a concept—unclear and invisible. Draw a picture for them, particularly with an analogy or a metaphor, and your prospects suddenly see; they understand.

You can't just build better mousetraps. You must draw pictures of them so that people can understand how your traps might snare more mice.

Seeing is believing and believing leads to buying.

Make yourself and your differences seen.

Boiled Critter at Tiffany's

She became the Aristocrat by wearing pearls—and not the other way around.

In a nutshell, that is the story of CBS. Media-wise observers know the company as the Tiffany Network—the premier, premium-priced service in its industry. How did it get there?

Pearls.

To confirm this, recall the 1960s or relive them by watching Nick at Nite. What do you see? You see the programs that catapulted CBS to the top of the Nielsens: *Petticoat Junction, Hee Haw* and *The Beverly Hillbillies*. You see Jethro and Elly May and a jalopy straight from *The Grapes of Wrath*.

You see hayseeds.

How could CBS air *Hee Haw* and still become known as broadcasting's Hope Diamond? Enter the pearls.

The pearls are those delicate white lights you see in downtowns every winter, flickering on the trees in front of large buildings. Who invented them? CBS, who surprised and impressed passersby in the early 1960s by draping those lights on the trees outside its midtown Manhattan headquarters.

The pearls complemented the basic black that CBS has just begun wearing—its famous headquarters still known as Black Rock. The architect Eero Saarinen, working with CBS's equally fastidious president, Frank Stanton, created Black Rock by defying the prevailing design of that era—the glass box—and designed instead a building that seemed to have been sculpted from black granite.

Like other CBS projects during Stanton's reign, the granite could not be just any granite. Saarinen searched the world for the right stone, which he finally found one day in northern Quebec.

Knowing that he was selling the invisible—airtime for advertisers—Stanton obsessed over CBS's visibles.

Even letters from CBS headquarters revealed this attention to detail. If, for example, you received several letters from CBS and placed them side by side on your desk, you noticed their distinctively neat blocks of copy, each identical in shape and size. If you held a letter to the light and looked closely, you would discover the secret—and the extent of Stanton's obsessiveness.

CBS's designers ensured that each copy block would match by making certain that each block started at the same spot. The designers had embedded a tiny, almost invisible gray dot on each page, one inch from the left margin and 2.25 inches from the top. Then they sent out a note instructing all CBS typists to begin the first word at precisely that point.

Not long after this memo went out and Black Rock went up, CBS demonstrated the extraordinary power of perception. Trade magazines began calling it "the Tiffany Network." Media reps began scheduling better restaurants for meetings with CBS network executives.

Just as significantly, CBS began believing its own image. Its employees became convinced they had the best programming, the best people, the best softball team T-shirts. CBS began wearing pearls, and soon, so did the employees behind it.

CBS became its image.

The *reality* at CBS was Jed Clampett and tattered coveralls. The *perception,* however, was black granite and snowy pearls, and perfect little letters all in a row. The image won. It trumped the reality—as images, especially in a business of intangibles, so often do.

We encourage people to dress for the job they want, rather than the one they have. On a larger scale CBS's triumph suggests you should dress like the company you wish to become, and that images do not merely create perceptions, but create realities.

In our hectic world, the sound bite has replaced the paragraph as the unit of thought. Our new world demands a faster message. So it is with your images— including the space in which you work—that you communicate to the world. Your logo, building, and lobby are your visual sound bites. Make them compelling and professional.

Clients love with their hearts, to be sure, but that love starts in their eyes.

Dress like the company you want to become.

What Your Space Says to Your Client

"The public relations firms around here are notorious," the marketing executive observed, "for building these over-the-top offices to impress clients. I'm not sure all that showiness works." ("Here" was Warsaw, Poland. Businesses are the same the world over, it seems.)

Does the fancy office work?

Or do clients view these showplaces as their money going up in teak and Aeron chairs?

These questions, it turns out, misunderstand the total effect of an office. An impressive office does not cause visitors merely to marvel at the firm's taste and budget. Visitors look around and sense that they have arrived, too. They feel they are where they belong; they feel important.

One of the world's leading wealth management firms carefully avoids extravagance in its interior design. Yet look carefully and you will notice the subtle but impressive Chippendale chairs, Waterford ice buckets, and other seemingly more expensive than necessary touches that remind its clients that they are special.

Your space—a key element of your packaging— does more than project how special you are. It reminds your clients how special *they* are.

Watch your space.

No Room at the Bottom

Aetna hammers on price, tries to squeeze the costs out of health care—and finds itself with a profit less than half its industry average.

A superstore moves in to Tampa and San Mateo, and a dozen discount retailers in each town soon close their stores forever.

Taco Bell charges pennies for its tacos, yet battles to survive.

In virtually every market, why is it that several companies known for reliability thrive, yet only one company known for low prices ultimately survives? Why is the low-cost niche so tiny?

Because of who we are and what we love.

Let's assume that our primary criterion for choosing a temporary agency is reliability. A trusted friend recommends the local office of AccuStaff. "They delivered what we needed when they promised."

Do you look further? Do you try to find your area's *most* reliable temporary service? Would you know that service when you found it? Could you be confident, even if you found the "most reliable" firm, that its most reliable people would be assigned to work with you?

No, no, no, no. You pick AccuStaff. They sound very reliable; that's good enough.

Now, switch criterion and assume that price drives your decision. You talk to AccuStaff and get their quote, which seems good. Do you stop there and choose AccuStaff?

You don't. You keep looking for the *best* price.

Price shoppers operate from this mentality: They want the best deal—and by definition, there is only one best deal. As a result, the rock-bottom firm can thrive. Everyone else loses, as Kmart, Montgomery Ward, Jamesway, Bradlees, and dozens of other low-priced retailers have learned. (By the beginning of this century, Taco Bell's new president no longer referred to Taco Bell's famous 99 cent prices as the chain's "point of difference." He called them "Our 99 Cent Trap.")

If you position yourself in one of the Power Positions—reliability, or innovation, for example—you can compete with other firms known for those traits. Several "reliable" or "innovative" firms can thrive. If you try to compete on price, only the lowest firm ultimately wins.

If you cannot get to rock bottom, or do not want to—a wise choice—stake another position. Low price won't work.

Resist aiming low.

Laid-Back Heart Surgeons and Other Horrors

When you seek someone to heal your pain, do you want them to be casual?

When you look for someone to repair your broken filling, instruct your children, or repair your car, do you want them to be relaxed?

When your cat is sick, your investments are plummeting, or your business is threatened by a lawsuit, do you seek out a casual veterinarian, a hang-loose investment manager, or a laid-back lawyer? Do you want service providers to be casual about your needs, relaxed about your time, and dressed as if they wished they were in Palm Springs instead of with you?

You don't.

Neither do your prospects.

If you're dressed for golf, be sure you're golfing.

But It Helps Recruitment

The career Web site Wetfeet.com asked business students to rate the importance of thirty-five job attributes.

"Ability to dress casually" finished last.

Casual policies attract casual employees.

Some Help from Hong Kong

"No one ever had a good idea," you may have heard, "wearing a tie." (The light bulb—the symbol of a great idea—must have been an ordinary idea. Thomas Edison wore ties even when mowing his lawn.)

Advocates of casual attire insist that comfortable people work better, which prompts this response: If your professional clothes feel uncomfortable, change clothes. Khaki pants feel like something to wear while traipsing through jungles—the purpose for which they were first designed. Tailored wool slacks, on the other hand, feel like pajamas.

To make yourself more comfortable and more appealing to prospects, go to a search engine and type in "Hong Kong tailors." Check out their Web sites and learn which tailors visit the city nearest you. When those tailors come to town, go to their hotel room and get measured for a dark jacket (150 superfine wool feels best), two pairs of dark pants, and two Egyptian cotton shirts.

These clothes will last twice as long as an affordable domestic suit and decades longer than your khakis. The pants and jacket will feel like skin and make you feel more at ease. Friends will ask, "What have you done to yourself?" Acquaintances will insist that you look fabulous. Your clients will be impressed but not overwhelmed.

Perhaps most remarkably, you will ultimately pay several hundred dollars less for your clothes because cheaper ones wear out just hanging in your closet.

Your initial investment in this comfortable and professional-looking perfection?

Less than $800.

To feel more comfortable, dress better.

Just Junk It

Never mind that Americans dislike direct mail so much they call it junk. Many people persist in the belief that something as measurable and relatively cheap as direct marketing must be effective.

But impersonal communications that violate people's boundaries—letters, calls, or e-mails to their home, their most sacred boundary—do not merely fail to generate adequate business. They can reduce it.

Mass efforts often fail for the very reason that makes them attractive: their efficiency. Efficient means cheap—and compared to most forms of marketing, mass communicating looks cheap. That's the problem; as Marshall McLuhan famously observed, "the medium is the message." A cheap medium conveys a cheap message of a cheap company.

Good marketing, among other things, communicates that you are good at what you do. Efficient marketing efforts brand you, too.

As second-rate.

Cheap efforts produce cheap results—or worse.

AMERICANS THE BEAUTIFUL AND *PRETTY WOMAN*

Caring Service

KEY TREND:
THE WISH TO CONNECT

"Even introverts need people. Adults invented work so they could keep playing together."
> —Silver Rose

When you buy a product, you purchase something tangible. When you buy a service, however, you buy the people who perform it.

You buy a hair stylist, for example, not a hair salon. Ask several experienced salon workers what their clients really buy, and each will say clients buy the almost therapeutic relationship with their stylist.

You buy products based on your feelings about the product; you choose your services based on your *feelings* toward the providers.

To test this, examine your favorite services. Are you loyal to the clinic where your favorite doctor works? Not at all. You are loyal to the doctor. If she changes clinics, you will, too.

Services resemble loving relationships. The best ones, in fact, *are* loving relationships. Minneapolis parents love Janice Eaves, who cares—literally and figuratively—for their children. Many San Diegans love Ophelia, Sharon, and the other wizards at Gary Greenberg's dental offices. Travelers worldwide adore Leftheris Papageorgiou of Hellenic Adventures, who leads them on tours of Mykonos, Santorini, and Turkey.

We love people, not institutions.

Our relationships with the people providing our service determines our perception of their service. The architect Frank Lloyd Wright, for example, became legendary for masterpieces like Fallingwater. But like many gifted professionals, Wright could offend anyone, and often did. He was difficult to like and almost impossible to love. As a result, this recognized genius spent much of his career searching for his next commission.

> *"The capacity to care gives life its deepest meaning."*
>
> —*Pablo Casals*

The more we like a person, the more capable that person seems. Think of the first person you truly loved. Remember how smart, witty, talented, and attractive that person seemed at the moment you fell? The truth is, that person possessed all those traits—in your eyes. Your warm feelings fogged up your glasses.

The successful business evokes those feelings—and the deeper the feelings, the better the business. *Great businesses connect.*

The New Communities

Only a hundred years ago people lived differently.

Families comprised more than two generations and children worked with their fathers. Prosperous families built second homes on the lake—but the lake was just three miles from the city center. Even when families left for the weekend, they barely moved.

Life was local. The globe was an exotic sphere in the living room. To a young man living near Cannon Beach, Oregon, San Francisco might as well have been Singapore. The map said that only seven hundred miles separated those two towns, but they occupied two different worlds.

Where are we now?

Everywhere. People come and go. Austin booms and Texas-bound flights are filled for weeks.

We once had town meetings. Now we use the term to describe televised conversations involving presidential candidates. With few exceptions, townspeople no longer meet. Cities that once had a town square now have Town Square—the name often given to a shopping center in the suburbs, not the town, as if to compound the irony.

This gap creates your opportunity. The company in this evolved economy seeks ways to create a community of its clients. Bring yours together—for seminars, open houses, or other excuses to gather. Add to your Web site a message board where clients can compare notes and solve problems. Invite them to contribute to your newsletter.

Connecting your clients will help connect them to you.

To connect with your clients, make connections for them.

Starbucks' Key Insight

Howard Schultz was nutty enough to think people will associate a mermaid with coffee, foolish enough to lavish millions on tiny product stickers, and shrewd enough to see that the ideal location for a business is at an intersection of change.

So he invented Starbucks.

Howard saw that the town squares were gone and their putative replacements, the malls, were teeming with suburbanites who rarely communed. He knew firsthand that in downtown Seattle and every other American downtown, almost everyone seemed to come from somewhere else.

Howard thought about this implosion and two images kept emerging. One was a classic image of both Paris and Milan: Parisians and Italians sitting at sidewalk tables, sipping, nibbling, and chatting. Even on cool days, people in Paris endure long waits to sit at outside tables so tightly packed that only Parisian waitresses—among the world's most petite—can maneuver between them.

Is it the weather and fresh air?

Only partly. A deeper reason for the popularity of sidewalk tables is their communal nature. Sitting at one, you see not just the other diners, but the thousands of people who walk by. You get a clearer idea of your community and of your place in it. You see where you live.

Schultz understood this and recalled another vivid image: the old Beat generation coffeehouses.

These spots died young. (It may've been the poetry.) But from the mid-1950s to early 1960s, these coffeehouses became American icons, featuring bongo drummers and goateed men reciting free verse while audience members sipped espresso as thick as black bean soup.

The Beat coffeehouses and European cafés answered the same need. But Americans had fewer sidewalk cafés—weather, zoning ordinances, and health codes all discouraged them. Yet the restaurants that tried sidewalk cafés—conspicuously, those in the Upper East Side of Manhattan and the Gaslamp District in San Diego—realized they answered a human need for something more than lunch.

So Schultz leapt into this void and created Starbucks, the sidewalk café and beatnik coffeehouse merged into one. (You can see how much Starbucks aspires to sidewalk-caféness at its shops like the one in Pioneer Square in Portland, Oregon. The shop is literally on the sidewalk, and resembles Philip Johnson's Glass House, its walls almost entirely glass.)

To make his shops profitable, however, he faced a hurdle: How do you build a thriving business charging $1.50 for each of a series of labor-intensive transactions?

The answer is, you don't charge $1.50. You charge more than twice that much.

You charge $3.75 for a cup of coffee?

How?

By realizing two basic principles. First, a service always involves more than the exchange of something tangible for money. You must build more into a service—warmth, connection, friendship, rest, status, and, in Schulz's case, community. People will pay extra for a feeling of community.

> *"Sociability . . . is necessary for human survival. Adults who isolate themselves from the world are more likely to die at comparatively young ages. We have a central dependence on others."*
> —Dr. John J. Ratey,
> *A User's Guide to the Brain*

Second, Starbucks spotlights the importance of status. Americans tend to identify themselves and stake their positions with items—from Hermès scarves to Volkswagen Jettas—that social scientists refer to as "positional objects." Anyone can afford a buck for a cup of Joe. But who can easily part with $3.75?

Someone special; coffee becomes a positional object.

"I am special," Starbucks customers sense when they buy their tiny luxury—as Schultz knew they would. In a complex and cluttered world, a Starbucks cup markets more than Starbucks.

It markets its drinker.

The need for community and the need for status intersected at that moment, and Schultz located his coffee stores there—and flourished.

Study Starbucks.

What Your Clients Actually Buy

His story could borrow its title from Theodore Dreiser's *An American Tragedy*. Possessed of virtually all the skills, my friend started a business, grew it— and killed it.

He had every skill but one: He did not understand what people buy.

Because he provided an expert service, he assumed people bought his expertise. But relatively few businesses—securities analysis, forensic science, a few others—are Expertise Businesses. The rest of us—from gynecologists and IT consultants to massage therapists and hair colorists—sell something else.

We sell satisfaction.

The French Laundry, considered one of the world's best restaurants, does not just sell Thomas Keller's magic with food. This Napa Valley restaurant sells three hours of satisfaction of which the spectacular food is just a part.

Lowry Hill, the wealth management affiliate of Wells Fargo, does not sell return on investment. It sells ease. Its partners will do anything, even call for front-row *Aida* tickets, to make its clients' lives easier.

Progressive does not sell car insurance. It sells comfort: the comfort of knowing that if you have an accident, they will be at the scene, ready to write a check.

ServiceMaster does not sell cleaning. It sells confi-

Like most enterprises that achieve cult status, the French Laundry sells more than just being there. It sells the experience of having been there. For the rest of their lives, French Laundry guests can discuss their experience with other foodies, and find common ground and animated conversation. The experience also confers status on the diner. Having dined at the French Laundry marks a person as sophisticated, discerning, serious about craft and quality—not to mention prosperous enough to afford $900 for a dinner for four.

dence. Its customers feel sure they will be treated well because of the company's passionate mission to live by the Ten Commandments.

Lawyers, architects, financial planners, accountants—no matter how well trained they are, few professionals sell their expertise.

They sell satisfaction.

A threshold level of skill gets these firms into their prospects' doors. But it is their apparent ability to satisfy clients that sells them, and their actual ability to satisfy clients that turns clients into loyal fans.

So what happened to my friend? He failed because he'd mastered his craft, but couldn't return a phone call. His peers envied his skills but his clients barely understood him. They took his lack of social skills personally and decided that he didn't like them, then responded as we all do. They stopped liking him, too.

Your business is not performing your task brilliantly.

It is satisfying your clients deeply.

Your task is not to perform; it's to satisfy.

A Lesson from Hong Kong

A revealing story from a perfect setting.

Scene One: The famous lobby café of Hong Kong's Peninsula Hotel, considered one of the world's great hotels.

Act One, Tuesday lunch: I order a salad and espresso, which arrive promptly. I eat, then hand the waiter my Visa card. He leaves. I sit.

More minutes pass: three, four, six, nine. I considered the irony that it is I, not the waiter, who is waiting. Ten, eleven, tw— No, I spot the waiter! He is delivering coffee four tables away. Surely he will notice me!

Well, no; he darts away again.

I feel torn. I want to appear proper and polite in this elegant setting, and I want to stand on my chair, windmill my arms like a cheerleader, and bellow "Over Here! Over Here!"

Wait, the waiter notices! He apparently remembers me from earlier this afternoon—hours ago, wasn't it? He hurries out the lobby and back in, carrying my card and credit slip. Waiter's elapsed time from taking my card to returning: fifteen minutes.

Act Two, Wednesday lunch: Convinced that my previous day's lunch was an anomaly, I return to the café. Within minutes the lobby is filled with a noise rarely heard in any hotel, much less a great one: a jackhammer. I tell myself the pounding will cease in seconds.

It does not. It continues. And continues.

And continues for more than twenty minutes. Many

other diners, who no doubt shared my confidence the racket would end fast, are laughing, presumably in amazement. Our ordeal appears to be over. I signal the waiter and boldly hand him my Visa card again. I realize he's the same waiter from the day before.

Yes: an encore performance of *The Disappearing Waiter*.

Ten minutes later, the waiter returns with my check, cut by at least half for all the diner's inconvenience, of course.

Well, no. The jackhammer apparently was entertainment. It must have been, because something is missing: an apology. No "Sorry for the noise and inconvenience." No "We have no idea how this could happen." No nothing except a large bill for a small lunch.

If the Peninsula, which many consider one of the world's premier service providers, failed this miserably on consecutive days with the same guest, how good are the merely good providers?

If the best services perform this badly, how good is your service—really?

Act Three: Three weeks later, the *Wall Street Journal* runs a front-page article about hotels' efforts to please their frequent visitors. A Hilton executive explains why hotels are spiffing these "road warriors."

"Everyone is looking for some way to stand out. We all have nice rooms. We're all in good locations." Then, his stunning kicker:

"*All* hotels have great service."

Had he visited a hotel recently?

Here's what hotels—which still are America's best service industry—might consider instead:

1. When a guest requests a wake-up call, two

morning papers, and a rush pressing of some slacks, send him a wake-up call, the two papers, and the pressed slacks—instead of just the pants; and

2. Encourage check-in clerks, when a guest mentions he has been standing in line for twenty-five minutes, not to say "Well, we are very busy today." Especially when that staff knew a year ago that the hotel would be filled that night.

Even the world's best hotels often fail dismally. Average hotels fail even more often, and yet the Hilton executive says that all hotels have great service.

He says it because we all suffer from Service Myopia. We believe our service is great. We all are worse than we think.

We all can, and must, get better.

Every service needs fixing.

An Insight from *The Great Gatsby*

Few forces drive us more than finding our place in the world. We love respect, regard, and esteem from others. The lust with which some people pursue wealth and others fame, in the end, can be traced to this desire.

We want to matter.

Lajos Egri, a teacher of fiction writing, once advised his students to recognize that a central force in every great novel is each character's sense of importance. You cannot miss that force when you read what many consider the Great American Novel, F. Scott Fitzgerald's *The Great Gatsby*.

Gatsby works relentlessly to become a man to be reckoned with, so that Daisy Buchanan will love him. Daisy wages her own battle to be respected, in her case by her husband, Tom, to whom no one but Tom matters. We see the entire story through Nick Carraway, a character with whom readers identify. Nick lives among the glamorous rich as an outsider, a mere bond salesman with a modest summer cottage among the mansions of East Egg. Although Nick deplores Daisy's and Tom's recklessness and arrogance, he craves their acceptance.

Nick wants to matter.

We all do.

Whenever you try to satisfy a client, this feeling dominates the transaction: that person's need to feel important.

A quick illustration. The next time you find yourself standing in a line when a customer explodes over some failed service—a muffed airline reservation or an order that never comes, for example—study that person.

Is he hating some inconvenience? Frustrated by a bad day? Concerned about paying for something he did not receive?

No. The customer feels upset because he feels slighted. He is not raging because the clerk did not care enough about her job. *He is raging because she did not care enough about him.* He is not concerned about convenience or cost.

He is concerned about himself.

Customers take customer service mistakes personally; these mistakes are about them. In the customer's view, the clerk did not err; instead, the clerk did not care—about the customer.

Nurture every client's sense of importance.

Americans the Beautiful: Understanding Positive Illusions

"What is an American?"

Frenchman Hector St. John de Crèvecoeur asked that famous question in the 1780s, a question that today holds some answers to another question:

Just who is your prospect?

Historian David Potter offers an intriguing answer in his award-winning book, *People of Plenty*. Potter concluded that Americans are what they have: unique among all people, Americans live with abundance. America's breadth and wealth have helped create a distinctive personality for its people and help explain democracy and our two-party system, Bill of Rights, and famous ingenuity. That abundance in turn has shaped our sense of ourselves. We feel special—so special, in fact, that social scientists coined a term for our self-regard: American Exceptionalism.

A widely circulated story about Daniel Boone reveals how well Americans think of Americans:

"He could leap into the air higher, dive into the water deeper, and come out of it drier than any man alive."

We think we are special and blessed. We laugh when Garrison Keillor claims that in his fictional hometown of Lake Wobegon, "all the men are strong, all the women are pretty, and all the children are above average." Then we learn that Americans so tend to overrate themselves that psychologists devised a term for it.

They call it the Lake Wobegon Effect.

We feel so certain of our superiority that every Olympic Games inspires dozens of Americans to write letters to editors asking, "Why didn't we win more medals?" These letter writers begin with an obvious conviction: Americans are inherently better. If American athletes failed, someone must have tampered with their water at the Olympic Village—or this new generation is taking its blessings for granted and not working hard enough.

In the April 2001 Journal of Personality and Social Psychology, professors Michael Ross and Anne Wilson offer more evidence of people's positive self-image—what UCLA psychology professor Shelley Taylor calls "positive illusions." They found that most people feel that they are better today—more skilled, mature, interesting, everything—than they were in the past. In their grand view, however, only they were growing and improving. They felt their friends and acquaintances were not.

Exceptionalism makes prospects and clients feel entitled. We are the best, we have the best—we deserve the best. Fail an

American and he will feel snubbed; you have disregarded his importance. To satisfy the American client, you need patience, persistence, and a knack for letting things pass.

Anyone who questions how highly Americans think of themselves should eavesdrop on a dating Web site.

Everyone's looks are at least "very good" and a stunning number call themselves "stunning." They insist they are very intelligent and patient, extremely warm and thoughtful, and considerate. They laugh readily and often. They read regularly, avoid fast food, and enjoy plays. They drink moderately and never too much, and few need to lose weight.

An observer can dismiss this self-praise as salesmanship, but if you look beyond it, you will see that in America, everyone is strong and good-looking and every child is above average.

America is Lake Wobegon. We are exceptional.

And we are your prospects.

Your clients think highly of themselves. You must show that you do, too.

Watching *Pretty Woman*

In a key scene in *Pretty Woman,* Julia Roberts's character enters a chic Beverly Hills clothier in her work clothes. Unfortunately, she's a streetwalker. The clerk treats Julia's character like lint.

Enter Richard Gere's character. He quickly conveys

to the clerk that he can afford the entire block on which the store was built. Gere then outlines his expectations for the clerk's service:

"We're going to need some major sucking up here."

The clerk obliges while the movie audiences roar.

They laugh for this very reason: We think well of ourselves and detest any hint of a snub. We take "all people are created equal" seriously; no one is our superior. We view any display of superiority as "putting on airs"—a revealing phrase. It shows that we view any notion of another person's superiority as having no more substance than air.

Today's abundance only enhances our sense of importance and feelings of entitlement. And as our abundance increases—which it always has over time—entitlement will increase, and satisfying your clients will become more difficult.

The large majority of people who grow up in stratified societies with strong distinctions among classes also grow up without Americans' strong sense of equality and Exceptionalism. They do not learn to be treated as important or to expect it. This may help explain why service in a highly stratified country like Great Britain is notoriously dreadful. Only upper class Brits learn to expect special service, much less learn to request it.

To satisfy every client's sense of importance, you must improve constantly.

Uncertainty and the Importance Principle

Even perfect clients fear you. They fear you care more about yourself than about them.

If you do not return a client's call quickly, it means she did not matter enough for you to call sooner. She imagines you gaily chatting with your other more important clients, answering *their* questions, caring about *their* children's success in school, roaring at *their* jokes.

You don't call for weeks. Your client feels unimportant.

You cancel a meeting. He feels unimportant.

You misunderstand her request to send your proposal "next Friday." She meant this Friday. You made an honest mistake and sent it a week after she expected it.

She feels unimportant.

Whenever they are in doubt, your clients will see your behavior—and your view of them—in the worst light. You must eliminate that doubt at every chance. Dot i's, cross t's, reassure your clients that they are important to you—every chance you get.

Remember the importance of importance.

People Need People

If you saw this headline, you smiled:

"Looking for DSL Service? You know, the kind with people?"

This simple bus shelter ad worked because it spoke to our desire. We want service from people, not from machines.

We dislike recorded messages. Answer our calls, show your interest in helping us.

We do not want machines; we want accountability: someone to call when things go wrong. We do not want to hear that your systems are down; we no longer accept this. Install better systems.

We do not want broadcast faxes or other junk mail equivalents, from mass phone messages to mass e-mail announcements. When we want service, we want the kind that DSL ad recognized.

The kind with people.

We like a human touch—literally. Many servers in restaurants know, and many studies have shown, that if a server touches your arm, lightly and for just a few seconds, you will leave a bigger tip.

Eliminate electronic shortcuts.

Money Can't Buy
You Loyalty

"I Love New York"—perhaps. But "I Love My Airline"?

When you receive free upgrades and other repayments for enduring airline travel, you've benefited from a loyalty program—a program designed to reward frequent and "loyal" customers.

Every company should know its best customers and strive to retain them. Loyalty marketing often fails, however, because too many of its practitioners assume that people feel loyal to companies. They do not.

People feel loyal to people.

A large, institutionalized effort to segment your heavy users, unless you accompany that effort with a personal one, will not make your clients loyal.

It will only discourage them from fleeing.

The airlines illustrate this fallacy behind many loyalty programs. Despite more than a decade of loyalty marketing, this country's airlines now have the least loyal—indeed, the most actively hostile—clients in the world. The reason is simple: Airlines mistreat their customers.

The airlines mail out pamphlets with some coupons, drink tickets, and car rental discount certificates. How are these loyalty mailings perceived? The author of the mailing might just as well have begun by writing, "Here are some things we give to people who give us lots of money."

The entire mailing is a form letter: impersonal, transactional, transparent.

If the airlines wanted loyal customers, they'd apologize. Their executives would call their loyal customers and say, "We're sorry for the summer we put you through and appreciate you for sticking with us."

If you want personal loyalty, you must touch people personally.

Loyalty doesn't come from marketing. It comes from personal sacrifices. Don't mass-mail or bribe customers. Instead, serve them. Develop a specific Key Client Plan for the next twelve months. Identify your key clients— that 20 percent who, if you are typical, provide about 80 percent of your revenue. Specify what you will do to make each of those clients feel appreciated.

Then do it.

If you want loyal customers, address them— personally—and serve the best ones passionately.

Efficient Tools Aren't

You are John, and receive this enticing letter.

"Dear John: I miss you. Marcia."

Naturally you are curious. Your pluck the envelope from your wastebasket to learn more. You turn over the envelope and read the address line. Your heart falls.

The letter is addressed: "Or Current Resident."

Bizarre? Of course. Yet Marcia's letter resembles one that businesses send regularly. Able to "personalize" their mass communications, companies do. Account executive Marcia, leaving for a weekend of skiing, mass mails a notice of her vacation to clients, making each letter seem addressed only to the client.

Like all of us, John knows Marcia has sent a general message. What message did he receive?

"You are just one among many clients."

Worse, Marcia has used "customer-service-enhancing technology" to pretend that she has taken time for John. Marcia has communicated to John not just that he doesn't matter, but that she thinks he can be fooled.

And that she's happy to try.

In relationships, however, the first rule is : *It's the time that counts.* Not the note, the e-mail, or the call—it's the time behind each communication that the recipient values most.

> *"Relationships are the most powerful form of media today."*
> —*Pam Alexander, CEO, Alexander Ogilvy*
> *Public Relations, San Francisco*

As words have become cheaper, time—finite, slipping away, and seemingly shrinking—has become more valuable. Gestures that take time tell the other person "you really matter."

Efficient customer service tools tell them, "My time matters more than you."

It's the time that counts.

"Thank You, (Enter Client Name Here)"

Avoid mass anythings.

Resist, for example, sending the same holiday gift to every client. Never send a greeting with only a signature; sending nothing works better. People want to feel important and recoil from any gesture that implies they are just another face.

To make clients feel like someone, you cannot treat them like just anyone. Mass mail makes people feel inconsequential. Hand-written notes, on the other hand, work magic.

Take time. Write by hand.

The End of the Line

First we saw road rage, then air rage. Now we've got "register rage." That's when customers become so irritated in a checkout line that they explode.

Twenty years ago, Americans used their time waiting in lines to chat with each another. Ten years ago, those people started tapping their feet. Today they are blowing up.

People aren't waiting anymore.

We want it faster, faster, faster. America's Research Group reports that more than four in five women and nine of ten men have stopped patronizing a store because of its long lines. Yet few retailers have spotted this problem. Most point to their surveys, which seem to show customer satisfaction, and insist there is no problem.

You probably don't think that your delays bother your clients, either. But they do. People today feel rushed—even those who say they aren't. They communicate this impatience with their feet.

They walk away, forever.

How fast should you answer your phone? One ring (practice it). How quickly should you return a phone call? Ten minutes (practice and instill this practice, too). Answer an e-mail? Ninety minutes today; next year, an hour.

For decades, insurance companies assumed that their policyholders expected a response to a claim in about a week. Progressive stepped in, said that's too slow, and began sending claims representatives to accident scenes, often to write a check before the tow truck arrived. *Before*. That fast.

> *A signal that dissatisfaction with services is growing: The February 20, 2000, Wall Street Journal reported the emergence of Rage Number Four: Hotel Rage, brought on by overbooked hotels and undertrained staffs.*

Progressive's business exploded.

Get faster faster.

Kohl's Race to Clients' Hearts

Kohl's gets it.

Kohl's Corp. has thrived while other department store chains have stumbled, sending those others to spy on Kohl's in search of its secret.

Department store buyers quickly found the secret—or so they thought. Kohl's offers department store, brand-name merchandise at lower prices. The buyers figured that Kohl's could charge less because it's comparatively small (86,000-square-foot average) stores were half the size of other department stores, and were located in areas with lower rents.

These buyers were one-third right. Its stores' designs have contributed enormously to Kohl's success. It's not, however, the savings that these designs produce. It's the profits they generate.

The size *and* configuration of Kohl's stores make them uniquely appealing—because Kohl's stores offer something no one thinks about in a department store: Speed.

You walk in a Kohl's and walk around a wide oval around the store, with not more than five racks on each side of you. If you find what you want and want to get off this oval track, each store features a middle aisle that leads straight to the registers. Your walk through the entire floor—and almost all Kohl's stores are on one floor to speed your visit—covers less than five hundred yards. That's half the distance you walk in the average department store.

You might assume that its clean layouts, with just five racks per department and wide aisles taking space where added merchandise might be, reduce Kohl's revenue. Apparently, they must boost it. Kohl's average sales per square foot exceed Marshall Fields's by 20 percent and Dillard's by almost 100 percent.

If you still wonder if speed is what makes Kohl's so attractive, consider the inspiration for Kohl's store design:

Racetracks.

Clients treasure their time, and you will benefit if you treasure it, too.

What can your business do?

Encourage a policy of answering every phone before the second ring. Abbreviate every voice mail message. Make sure everyone's office phone rolls into their cell phone when they are away from their desks—and encourage employees to carry their cell phones whenever they are away.

Whatever you do, do it faster. Speed works.

As a trip by a Kohl's parking lot will tell you.

Shave seconds everywhere.

Despite its emphasis on low prices, Kohl's still understands the value of packaging. Its merchandise is arranged according to detailed research on customers' preferences in color patterns, and the store rigorously enforces a daily 2:00 P.M. "recovery period," where every Kohl's employee—including secretaries and store managers—straightens up its merchandise displays.

How Priceline Almost Snapped

Priceline.com seemed a breakthrough idea, a killer app for the Internet. Just go online and ask for your price on hotels, travel, and other services.

Priceline.com backed this idea with conspicuous and frequent television ads featuring actor William Shatner, best known for commanding *Star Trek*'s Starship *Enterprise*. For reasons that mystified many people, these ironic ads worked. People flocked to Priceline's Web site.

Once.

Priceline.com nearly killed itself with complexity. Its Web site was confusing and slow. People who valued their time—everyone—subconsciously began doing cost-benefit analyses while plodding through the site.

I got a good price, these customers said. But is this worth my time?

No.

Simplify and speed up everything. Start a Total Speed Initiative. Examine every prospect and client activity, and measure or estimate how long each act takes—the average number of rings to answer the phone, time taken to return a proposal or track down someone "away from their desk"—every step of your service.

Then cut the time in half.

Then cut it by half again until you near real time.

After hiring great receptionists, no initiative will do more to improve your client satisfaction.

Implement a Total Speed Initiative.

The Good Neighbors Drop By

For several American outsourcing companies, millions of dollars were at stake in the spring of 1998. Those millions belonged to one of America's largest insurance companies, State Farm, and were about to go to an outside firm to handle the insurer's payroll, benefits, and several other employee programs.

Each finalist presented well. Their brochures looked professional, their presenters seemed warm and trustworthy.

How did State Farm choose?

In the end—as often happens—these prospects were stumped. Who to choose? They devised a solution: They piled into their cars and, without calling ahead, visited the offices of each finalist.

They walked into the lobbies, greeted the receptionists, looked around, and briefly visited their contacts. Then they left, and decided. Who?

"We chose the company that felt the best."

State Farm's executives viewed pounds of proposals, hours of presentations, and some gee-whiz overheads. Then they—like thousands of prospects, including yours—chose the company whose lobby and receptionist "just felt right."

How does your space make people feel? Does it feel welcoming and professional?

Do the employees look like people with whom you would do business?

Your next great client could drop by this afternoon. Always be ready and always feel right.

The Mercer, the Morgan, and the Grand: The Power of Welcome

Some words work like potions: They alter how we feel.

Psychologists have found this true of many words, including one word of special value to service providers: *welcome*. That word reduces the heart rate and anxiety of people who hear it.

Petting a cat has the same influence, as another successful service provider has learned. The Wild Rumpus bookstore in Minneapolis, a children's bookstore so popular that *Fortune* magazine once tried to uncover its secrets, features cats roaming the store and sunning like sultans in the front window. (If your service is informal, maybe you don't need better ads. You need more kittens.)

Guests at the Grand Bar in New York's SoHo Grand Hotel have witnessed the magic of *welcome* for years. They enter the bar and are warmly greeted by a striking woman named Tracy—so warmly, in fact, that they linger longer, spend more, and recommend Tracy's bar to everyone: a New York bar where everyone smiles at you— you must see it!

In our work, we have learned that the first five seconds—the greeting, the welcome, the receptionist's answer—influence customer satisfaction more than any other act. Clients love feeling welcome.

How do you greet prospects and customers?

How do people answer your phones? Are they welcoming? Or do they answer like the former receptionist of a large New York accounting and consulting firm? An executive of that firm once answered a questionnaire that asked, "How are callers and visitors to your firm greeted?" with the scrawled response,

> *The wizard behind the Grand and many other overflowing New York bars—the Mercer, Morgan, the Whiskey, and Whiskey Blue—Randy Gerber, confesses that his first priority is finding friendly servers. (Mr. Gerber is also famous, at this writing, for being Mr. Cindy Crawford.) "I tell all my employees that you can go and buy a Heineken at the bar next door," Gerber told Soho Style magazine in 2000. "Customers may come once because they've read about a place. But if they come back a second time, it's because of our staff."*

"By a curt and rude receptionist!"

Master the welcome.

Your Fastest Way to Improve Client Satisfaction

Hit the streets.

Ask six people—ideally, six employees—to spend the next four weeks noticing every receptionist they encounter, and ask each to bring back the best one's name.

Then arrange to meet those six receptionists. Select your two favorites, call each one, and offer the person with the warmest telephone greeting a 30 percent salary increase to work for you.

Executives at Banfield (formerly VetSmart) discovered from thousands of customer surveys that its first seconds with its clients—its welcome—influences client satisfaction more than any other act of customer service.

The welcome is the magic moment in customer service.

During your new receptionist's first week, you'll notice something different: the tone of the people who call you. Your new receptionist will

A service that understands the power of a great receptionist is the Ohio State University Alumni Association in Columbus, Ohio. Its wonderful receptionist greets people warmly, partly because her business card constantly reminds her of her enormous influence. Her title on it reads, "Director of First Impressions."

Richard Stern, the longtime receptionist for the Greater Phoenix Economic Council, has earned a broader title that reflects a receptionist's influence. His title is "Director of First and Last Impressions."

have warmed each call, and made your life easier—
and your conversion rate higher.

**To make your reception remarkable, find—
and pay for—a remarkable receptionist.**

Four Rules for
Choosing Clients

Trust your instincts. If something feels wrong, it
will be.

Bad clients don't produce minimal returns; they
produce losses.

If a prospect is most interested in cost, you will
never be happy and always be vulnerable.

**You cannot cut a bad deal with a good person
or a good deal with a bad person.**

The Gift That Isn't

Try to imagine the glee of the several hundred American executives who, on the Monday after Thanksgiv-
ing last year, found a paperback-sized box on their
desks.

Imagine their face-filling smiles when they opened

the boxes to discover their surprise: Chocolate, in the shape of a thick, number 10-sized envelope!

Picture their looks of glee when they studied their chocolate envelope, noticed a raised area in the upper-left-hand corner, and realized it was the logo of a direct mail company they recently had used for a project.

Now, imagine their feeling. "This company appreciates me so much that they send me an *advertisement*?"

Send gifts and advertise, but never at the same time.

Watch what you give.

Your Clients Were Always Right

"Now, let me tell you about this client we had."

No, let's not. Never say anything about a past client that might be heard as criticism.

Those statements threaten prospects and clients. They make them worry that you will criticize them, too.

Praise all clients—especially past ones.

Keeping a Client's Confidence

A Spanish proverb says it perfectly:

Whoever gossips to you will gossip about you.

Never divulge anything about a client that may appear confidential. Protect—and appear to protect—every client, past and present, a rule that springs from a truth every person knows:

People who reveal secrets will reveal ours.

Keep your client's secrets.

A Promise Written Is a Promise Kept

"An oral promise isn't worth the paper it's written on," someone once wrote, and there's business wisdom in that wit.

Consider an all-too-common occurrence. You say that you will meet Susan at Picasso at 3:30 tomorrow afternoon. At 2:45 that afternoon, your phone rings. "Where are you?" Susan asks. "Right here, I said I'd be there at 3:30." "No," she tells you. "You said 2:30."

The Gosh Answer always follows. In a tone that suggests you think she might be right (you know she isn't), you say, "Gosh, I could have sworn I said 3:30."

And on this conversation goes—too often—all over the world.

For purposes of growing your business, Susan is always right in these occurrences. She's disappointed and frustrated, and she's lost something precious: time.

There's a way to minimize these mistakes—and perhaps even better to avoid being blamed for them. Every time you offer to do something for a client—*anything*—write it down. Then send the client a copy, so you both will know just what was promised.

Keep your promises organized by date. That will allow you to scan your desktop, computer or conventional, and see your key dates.

What if you believe you made no promises? Write that down, too. Send it, and ask your client to confirm that that is her understanding, too.

There are few things that clients value more than consistency and predictability, the comfort of knowing that you will do just what you said—as they heard you say it. In this case, your mere oral promises aren't worth the paper you failed to write them on—but your written promises are worth thousands.

Put every promise in writing.

Your Three Key Moments: 3, 24, 5

Is there is a shortcut to superior service? No. There are three.

First, master the 3. Research constantly shows that the first three seconds influence client satisfaction more than every minute of service that follows. How do you greet people? What immediate impressions does your office make? Is the visitor greeted immediately and warmly? Does the receptionist's desk face the people who enter your office?

Are your phones always answered within three rings, and warmly? Is your office alive? (To help create that impression, put a vase of fresh flowers on the receptionist's desk—a powerful influence, it turns out.)

Now, the 24. Bell South learned this "Lesson of 24" vividly. Studying two customer service groups for its commercial clients, Bell South managers found that Group One enjoyed a 40 percent higher rate of customer satisfaction than Group Two. For weeks, they couldn't figure out why. Then, the discovery.

Group One had a written policy that required employees to follow up with their clients within twenty-four hours of a call, visit, or engagement with a simple message. "Is everything okay?" "Did you get the (information/answers/service) you needed? Is there anything more we can provide you?" Follow up within twenty-four hours. Always.

Finally, the 5. (You'll need twice as many envelopes

this coming year.) Five days (plus or minus one) after a significant prospect or client contact, send a thank-you. And you'll need more pens, too, because you should handwrite the note. Word-processed notes are too easy to create from a template and easy to delegate to a secretary. Handwritten notes clearly show that the person was worth your time.

To develop the habit, carry thank-you cards and envelopes everywhere. Planes, coffee shops, restaurants while you're waiting for your lunch date. The opportunities occur constantly. (An added plus: Note-writing is more interesting than any inflight magazine and 90 percent of all airline menus.)

3, 24, and 5: These moments work magic, and build businesses.

Understanding Listening

"We listen."

Everywhere today, companies are promising prospective clients that they listen. If they were listening, however, they'd know better than to say that—and know the real reason that listening matters to clients.

The overuse of this claim has rendered it useless. If anything, making the claim without any supporting evidence makes it suspicious, just as a common claim by attorneys aroused the fears of people like the late Sam Ervin, the senator who became famous as chairman for the Watergate hearings.

"When someone tells me he's just a 'humble country lawyer,'" Ervin said, "I immediately reach back and make sure I still have my wallet."

Companies that promise "we listen" make a second mistake, which they reveal almost immediately. With few exceptions and only slight changes in wording, all of them continue, "We listen carefully to you and then tailor a solution that will meet your specific needs."

This suggests that few companies realize why clients value people who listen. It's not because listening increases the chances of getting a better solution. Three studies over the last ten years—from the nation's leading commercial developer, the Upper Midwest's large law firm clients, and the VIP Forum—demonstrate that clients do not buy solutions. In each survey, "responsiveness to phone calls" and "sincere interest in developing a long-term relationship" ranked significantly higher in importance than "technical skill"—the ability to devise the best solution.

It isn't the better solution that clients value. It's the simple act of listening itself. We value it because of how it makes us feel. It makes us feel important.

Test your experience. You meet someone at a party, for example, and he displays all the traits of the chronic nonlistener. His eyes dart around the room. He begins speaking the second you stop, often on a new topic. He doesn't engage you with his body, moving close—"listening with the entire body."

What do you say about the person after the party? You say you weren't impressed; he seemed a bit full of himself. But you are only devaluing him because he devalued you. He made you feel unimportant.

Everywhere, we seek esteem, and seek to avoid the situations that diminish us. This makes us avoid people who seem not to value us; we avoid services that do not listen.

You must listen. Your business depends on it.

Your Silence Is Golden

The speaker strides to the podium and surveys the crowd. Two seconds, three seconds, four. Finally, with everyone in the audience now watching attentively, she speaks.

A singer stops and the music plays. Five seconds, then ten, now more. You feel the suspense as you wait for what she will sing next.

A witness waits seconds before answering the DA's question. You listen far more carefully than you would if the witness had replied immediately.

Silence—the pregnant pause, the white space of conversation—works. It brings the words around it into higher relief. It suggests those words will matter. It makes those words affective and more memorable.

In selling and marketing, it's hard to resist talking, enthusiastically and often. But that makes you appear too eager to sell and too inclined not to listen.

In 1981, E. F. Hutton surpassed $1 billion in assets. Every day, in thousands of television commercials, they reminded us that "When E. F. Hutton talks, people listen." Seven years later, E. F. Hutton was gone.

E. F. Hutton fell backward because they had it backwards. Clients will listen to you only after you show that you will listen to them.

Listen. Listen long, listen hard, listen and pause before you speak.

How to Listen

Don't just listen to what the person is saying. Picture it.

As he speaks, create a visual image—a movie, even—of his story. This will help you understand, follow, and remember his story—and even help you remember it a month later. It can help you remember that Sue Crolick's daughter Jessie is living in a well-worn Victorian near Haight-Ashbury in San Francisco, and that Jessie's boyfriend is training for the Olympics in the triathlon after switching from rowing. If you retained only the words of that story and not the images, you'd forget it the next day.

Don't listen with your ears. Listen with your eyes.

A Lesson from the Eastern Oregon Desert: How to Remember Names

Funny where you find the answers to problems. This one you can find at the home of Pendleton Round-Up.

Just one block north of the Great Pacific Wine and Coffee Company, which serves the best cappuccinos west of Milan and where much of this book was written, is Dean's Pendleton Sports, which Dean Fouquette has owned since graduating from the University of Oregon in the late 1970s. No doubt some of Dean's success can be traced to his celebrity status; he's the only Pendleton Buck player ever to be named All-State in three sports. But Dean also has a gift that clients love; he remembers everyone's name.

It's a trick.

Whenever he hears a person's first name for the first time, Dean immediately gives them a memorable last name—usually that of a famous person. So he never meets a Tom, Dick, Harry, and June. He meets "Tom Cruise, Dick Nixon, Dirty Harry, and June Bug." He also quickly finds some physical trait of his new acquaintances that matches his made-up name—Tom's teeth and Dick's nose, for example, or simply imagines that person as the made-up one—seeing Harry saying "Make my day," for example.

It works, because we remember distinctive words better than generic ones, and remember images better than words (as illustrated by the common phrase, "I remember the face but cannot place the name").

Try it. Few things sound as precious to another's ears as the sound of their own name.

Be like Dean.

The Rule of "Whole Plus One"

On October 13, 1994, a Marshall Field's clerk promised a Minneapolis customer that his summer-weight sport coat would be altered and ready by noon on October 23. The man appeared, but the coat did not; it wasn't ready. The customer appeared distraught, as most customers do when something promised isn't delivered—even though, in this case, it was something the customer didn't need (given Minneapolis weather) for at least seven months.

The clerk that day, an intense dark-haired man named Roger Azzam, sensed the customer's frustration and raced to the tailor's room, returning at high speed just seconds later. "Five minutes," Roger gasped to the customer. "We'll have it for you in five minutes."

Was the customer satisfied? That was only the beginning. He felt indebted. Roger, obviously a Type A living on the brink of a coronary, had all but risked his life over the customer's sport coat. The customer felt a moral obligation, and ten minutes later tried to discharge it—with $1,300 dollars' worth of clothes.

Roger had learned the power of the Reciprocity Principle, a lesson every service person should know.

The Reciprocity Principle holds that people keep tabs; we know what we've done for others, and they for us. We know "they've had us for dinner twice, and we've had them just once" for example. Hence, "it's our turn." We remember favors given and favors received, and most people know when they are running a deficit.

But the Reciprocity Principle does not dictate that you should merely make clients whole when you make mistakes. As Roger's sacrifice indicates, the great power lies in making a client "whole plus one."

To illustrate why "making the client whole" is not enough, consider another true and common story. A woman got a permanent from a Upper East Side New York salon. Three weeks later, she looked in her bathroom mirror and realized that her permanent had been only temporary. With her straight hair offered as proof, she returned to the salon. The salon offered "to make her whole"; they would refund the entire amount.

Did that woman feel whole and satisfied?

No. She got only the money she spent. She received nothing for her time spent going to and from the salon, in the chair, or suffering the frustration of not having what she wanted—never mind what she paid for. The refund only covered the woman's cost of money and neglected her costs of time and emotions.

Like every service, the salon needed to make the

customer "whole plus one." And your service must, too. To make a client who will come back—one who will actually use more of your services and pay more for them—you must overdo it.

Don't just undo your mistakes. Overundo them.

Ten Rules of Business Manners

Reread these regularly, and put a copy of them on every employee's desk. Living by these rules will make your business and life—yours and others— richer, in every sense of the word:

1. Always wait a split second after a person finishes talking before you speak.
2. Listen with your entire body.
3. Be positive.
4. Speak well of others.
5. Memorize names.
6. Never try to impress. The effort always shows, and it diminishes you.
7. Never make your conversations—particularly on cell phones—public.
8. Praise but never flatter. Praise makes people feel good; flattery makes them feel manipulated.
9. A simple rule whenever you are in doubt: Be kind.

Just do these.

Staff Like Spago

Hire for relationship, train for skill. There are two good reasons to follow this strategy.

First, people constantly grow at their tasks but few improve at relating.

And people forgive the mistakes of people who seem to care for them, but rarely forgive those who seem not to.

Wolfgang Puck's Spago Hollywood treated its customers splendidly. Puck created that level of service by hiring it, as Mimi Avins of the *Los Angeles Times* discovered. "Puck knew it would be easier to hire a nice person and teach him how to serve," Avins wrote, "than to try to make an experienced but nasty server pleasant."

Avins's story appeared in the Los Angeles Times, *Monday, March 19, 2001, to cover the closing of Spago Hollywood as Puck moved to focus his Los Angeles operations on his newer and larger Spago in Beverly Hills.*

Clients love people who care about them, and show it, and forgive them their trespasses, stumbles, and falls. Hire them.

Hire for relationships and train for skill.

Ritz-Carlton's Shortcut to Satisfied Clients

As you enter the front door the hotel bellman smiles. You enter the lobby and two maids pass by. They smile. You walk up to the desk to check in. The clerk smiles. Everywhere you go, people smile.

There are two possibilities. You are in *The Stepford Wives* or in a Ritz-Carlton hotel.

How do Ritz-Carlton hotels make you feel so welcome?

You might argue that it's their prices, which allow them to pay and attract the best employees. But that cannot be the answer; most hotels that charge more do not make their guests feel as welcome.

It is not the money at a Ritz-Carlton. It's the mantras.

Each day, each hotel employee receives a memo from the property's director of guest services. This information changes daily and weekly but one fixture never changes. Each communication offers the mantra of that day: one key service idea for every employee that day.

One day it may be "Remember each guest's name and use it often." The next day, "Tidy up anything that looks out of order." On that day you checked in, it read, "Smile at every guest and make each feel special."

After reading and practicing one mantra a day for day after day, the Ritz-Carlton mantras become practices and those practices soon become habits. Eventually those habits become part of the employee's way of thinking and working. The employees perform better, and then become better—more helpful and caring. Mantras change our actions, and then those actions change our attitudes. We become what we do.

"One does what one is; one becomes what one does."

—Robert Musil

This point deserves repeating. Too often we view pithy reminders as worthless clichés—perhaps because we notice that many people who utter them fail to live by them. This shouldn't distract you from recognizing this: Mantras *do* work. We repeat something and we begin to act upon it; we act in a certain way repeatedly, and we become that action—those powerful words become behavior and that behavior becomes us.

We do what we say, and then we become what we do.

Try mantras. They will transform the people who use them, and improve your service.

One shortcut: Use mantras.

How Judy Rankin Shot a 63

Addressing the crowd of women in March 2002, the pro was stumped. The World Golf Hall of Fame member and current television golf commentator Judy Rankin was encouraging more than 140 current LPGA players in the audience to reach out more to fans; however, she confessed she had no idea how. "I was never very good at that," she said.

Judy was implying that you have it, or you don't— the corollary of the "Natural Salesman," the glad-hander who can sweet-talk a penguin into buying a tuxedo.

The speaker couldn't resist. "Judy, your first round of golf, what did you score?"

"I was nine, I think. I shot an eighty-four."

"Eighty-four? For only nine holes? Judy?"

"Yes."

"You sucked!"

The speaker continued. "Now as a professional, what was your best score?"

"Sixty-three."

"Sixty-three—that's one-hundred-and-five strokes better for eighteen holes. A hundred-and-five! How'd you get so much better?"

"Hard work, persistence . . ."

"That's right, Judy—you *practiced*!"

The advice to the golfer was the same advice an aspiring writer received when he asked a famous author how to become a writer.

"Sit down and write something everyday," the author said. "Ten years from now, you'll be a writer."

Start practicing today. Choose one "best practice" and practice it every day, one practice at a time. Once you've mastered it, move to the next—like writing twice as many handwritten notes, learning to remember people's names, or looking people in the eye without scanning the crowd behind and around them. As simple as it sounds, just do it: practice.

Your words will become your behavior. Your behavior will become your habit. And your new habit will reward you. At the end of the year, everything will be different: you, those you touch, and your business.

Practice. Every day.

THE TRAITS
CLIENTS LOVE

HUMILITY AND GENEROSITY

Sean Bruner of Tucson likes movies, particularly director Julian Schnabel's 2000 release *Before Night Falls*. He liked Schnabel and the movie a lot more, however, before he read the March 25, 2001, *New York Times Magazine*.

In his letter to the publication's editor, Bruner revealed what clients love—and do not. "I do not understand," Bruner wrote about the March 25 article on Schnabel, "why Schnabel found it necessary to trash other films. *Cast Away* was not flawless, but it was good.

"Schnabel lowers himself in my esteem by attacking it."

With exceptions like Alice Roosevelt Longworth—who once said "If you can't say something good about someone, come sit by me"—we dislike people who criticize others, particularly those who disparage their competitors.

Ask the people at Deloitte Consulting.

In 1998, the firm decided to launch an ad campaign that capitalized on people's growing disenchantment with consulting firms. You could see this disdain in a flurry of books attacking these firms—with such titles as *Dangerous Company* and *The Witch Doctors,* which gave away the endings—and a wave of consultant jokes, highlighted by Matthew Diffee's March 26, 2001, *New Yorker* cartoon. The illustration showed two detectives standing over a lifeless body. "From the violent nature of the multiple stab wounds," one tells the other, "I'd say the victim was probably a consultant."

Deloitte's executives decided to capitalize on this hostility by running ads that tried to distinguish their firm from their rivals, whom they depicted as overpaid, impractical, and untested. As Sean Bruner might have predicted, Deloitte's campaign's bullet ricocheted and struck the firm.

The suicide wish in Deloitte's tactic can be suggested by a parallel campaign.

Imagine that you are a customer for dental services and you notice a dental office's ads that suggest that other dentists make their patient's mouths throb for hours. How does this ad make you feel? How eager are you to schedule a dental checkup? More important, how do you feel about the dentists who ran this disparaging campaign?

Deloitte's attack did more than assail its competitors. By targeting its own industry, Deloitte *attacked itself.*

The campaign tainted Deloitte. When asked how they felt about the firm,

In fairness to Deloitte, a good firm, its competitors often stumble, too. People worldwide have lambasted the name Accenture for what formerly was Andersen Consulting and cannot decipher its intended meaning, which Accenture executives say is their firm's accent on the future. This fails to distinguish the firm from any other. Meanwhile, Accenture's former colleagues at Arthur Andersen were violating the Rule of Humility (and the one against clichés) by running ads with enormous headlines that shouted, "The first name in professional services."

many readers of these ads said the firm was "petty, envious of bigger firms, desperate for work." The ads also bruised Deloitte & Touche, their affiliated CPA firm, both by association and by a common misperception that the accounting firm, not the consulting firm, had authored the ads.

Within weeks of the campaign's first appearance, a Deloitte representative began touring America to defend what he called the "Naming Names" campaign. (Had he thought about that title, he might have considered both his speeches *and* the campaign. As many readers know, the phrase "naming names" was coined during the communist witch hunts in Hollywood, which ruined the careers and reputations of many people who "named names.")

Just months later, Deloitte recognized its folly and called the speaker home, ending their assault on their competitors—and on themselves.

Never praise yourself or criticize a competitor.

Sacrifice

Romeo and Juliet is regarded as the world's greatest love story because it illustrates something that people love.

Everything in this play builds to the moment when Romeo discovers his seemingly lifeless Juliet. Overcome with grief, he stabs himself so that he might join her in death. Juliet then awakens from her drug-induced sleep and discovers that Romeo is dead. Overcome, she takes his sword and with it takes her life.

Death represents an extreme sacrifice; to be sure. But the play recognizes that a hallmark of a true relationship is sacrifice.

This rule applies—less dramatically, of course—to business.

Sacrifice and the idea of reciprocity—our inclination to feel obliged to return favors—are closely related. Robert Cialdini discusses several sales strategies that rely on reciprocity—most notably, the Hare Krishnas' successful efforts to solicit funds by offering copies of their valuable-looking books—in Influence: The Psychology of Persuasion.

Just after 5:00 P.M. one Saturday, a Seattle executive walked to his chest of drawers to fetch his cuff links. Unfortunately, the links were hiding under the bed in a hotel room where he had stayed two week earlier. Panicked by his vision of paper clip cuff links, he called Seattle's downtown Nordstrom store and explained his plight to a salesclerk.

The clerk had already planned her Saturday night. But when her customer called, duty called as well. She found some cuff links she knew he would love, closed up her register, jogged to her car, and sped to Mercer Island to deliver the links.

That drive transformed her customer into a lifelong friend. That man now goes out of his way to buy from Nordstrom, an act of almost perfect mathematical reciprocity: The clerk went out of her way; he now goes out of his.

You give me; I give back. You go beyond your call of duty and I will go beyond mine.

Sacrifices tell clients that you care, which makes them care more in return. Your sacrifice transforms the relationship. Now, you no longer are a service.

You are *their* service.

Give something up and you will get more back.

Openness

You reveal your intimate secrets only to people you trust deeply. In confiding in them, you do not merely communicate your secret; you express your trust. You are saying "You are special. I trust you with this secret."

Remember the last time someone acted as if she trusted you completely? How did you feel?

Wonderful.

In business as in life, people who reveal themselves—who admit mistakes or weaknesses, for example—communicate that they trust the person to whom they reveal themselves. They gain that person's appreciation in return. Revelations build the foundation of lasting relationships: trust.

Researchers at Cleveland State discovered this power some years ago, in a study mentioned in *Selling the Invisible*. They created two identical résumés and letters of recommendations for two fictitious job prospects, Robert and John. The first letter raved about Robert. John's letter was identical except for one additional sentence. The reference wrote, "John can sometimes be difficult to work with."

Personnel directors were most attracted to John, because they trusted John and his reference. They felt confident they could trust someone who so willingly allowed a shortcoming to be revealed.

Tell everyone the truth. Even when it hurts, it will assure clients that you will risk yourself to tell them the truth, and earn their trust—the foundation of every great relationship.

Reveal yourself.

Integrity and What It Actually Means

Clients love quality.

But in a service, what *is* quality?

The heart of a product's quality is its structural integrity. Rather than falling apart, the product stays together—it remains *integrated,* a word cognate with *integrity*. The integrity of its parts allows a product to perform.

The heart of service quality also is integrity—but the integrated elements are different. Your service is your promise that at some future date you will perform a task. The integrity in a service, then, is the integration between word and deed—between promise and performance. When your promises and performance match, you have integrity—something that clients want and need.

Integrity is quality. We inspect products before we buy them, eyeing them from every angle to ensure that they'll perform. When we inspect a service, we look for all the clues that will tell us the service will be performed as promised. To do that, we must look at the people promising the service and ask, "Do we believe them?"

We believe people who earn our belief; those who tell the truth, even when it hurts them. Their insistence on making sure that their words and actions are integrated makes them our trusted source.

When you tell the truth, people know what to expect. They feel more confident—a welcome feeling in this age of mistrust. They can rest assured and worry about something else.

> *The idea that quality in a service is measured by the relationship between what a service promises and what it performs explains why on any night McDonald's customers will say they are satisfied while customers at four-star restaurants—with much better food, service, and ambience—will say they were disappointed. McDonald's can deliver less and still satisfy its customers because it promises less. This reminds us that quality is not absolute, but relative; it is performance relative to promise. To ensure that you deliver quality, you must watch what you do and what you promise.*

> *"Always do right. This will gratify some people and astonish the rest."*
> —Mark Twain

Build integrity throughout your organization. Hire for it, reward it, demand, deliver, and tell it—fearlessly.

Integrity matters—and works.

What Clients Love Most

Ask loyal clients of any company why they remain loyal, and they will give one answer more than all others combined.

Do they mention excellence, quality, skill, or price? Not often.

They answer "comfort."

"Comfort" is what Adam Stenavich and several thousand other recruits answer when asked why they chose their respective colleges. It's what O. J. Oshinowo would answer to explain why Stanford appealed to him after he learned that one of its top professors of electrical engineering—O. J.'s planned major—was a fellow Nigerian.

The clients of excellent companies with records for quality—State Farm, Leo Burnett, Microsoft, and others—give that reason, too:

Comfort.

In this age of so many choices and messages, with trust declining and mobility and opportunity splitting communities and family connections apart, and with so many of our choices involving things we cannot see or inspect, today's client feels uniquely uncomfortable.

This means clients crave comfort more than anything.

How do you answer that craving?

Everything that precedes this section suggests steps to take. A familiar name and brand makes people comfortable; they feel more confident with a known name and brand.

Perceived expertness comforts people. Companies that look and sound expert—that look and dress professionally and appear often in newspapers and magazines—comfort this anxious client.

Clarity comforts. It helps people understand, which makes them more confident about who you are and why they should choose you.

Integrity comforts. It assures people that—in a world of considerable uncertainty—they can predict what you will do from what you say. That feeling is rare—and because it is rare, it is valuable.

Expressing your genuine interest in people comforts them, too. It assures them you will protect their interests as well as yours. It lays the foundation of trust—the centerpiece of a lasting relationship.

Even your passion comforts people. It shows you love what you do, which increases the chances that you will perform well. Passion comforts.

You love comfort, we love comfort, clients love comfort—comfort above all else. We admire excellence and envy superiority, but it is simple comfort that captures and keeps us.

Comfort clients and you will keep them.

YOUR GREATEST ASSET

Why do Some People and Businesses Thrive?

Historian David Landes recently asked that question about entire groups of people. He looked at entire nations, from Argentina to China, from Holland to Egypt. He pored over books, articles, and treatises whose titles filled sixty-seven pages of the bibliography to his book, *The Wealth and Poverty of Nations: Why Some Are So Rich and Some So Poor.*

Finally, Landes reached the conclusion—his, and his book's. Why *do* some people prosper?

The answer should resonate with all of us:

> *"In this world, the optimists have it, not because they are always right, but because they are positive. Even when they are wrong they are positive, and that is the way of achievement, correction, improvement, and success. Educated, eye-open optimism pays."*

The believers win. "They conquer," as John Dryden said, "who believe they can."

At about the time that Landes was finishing his book, David Pottruck and Terry Pearce were completing theirs—*Clicks and Mortar*—about another success. In less than twenty years, the authors asked, how did Charles Schwab evolve from a small discount brokerage to one of the world's most esteemed financial services firms?

It's in their hearts, the authors argued. More than great products, services, or prices, it was passion that propelled Charles Schwab—the man and his company—to greatness.

Yet another writer, historian Victor Hanson, was puzzling over a related question at this time. Hanson wondered how the United States, which had tried so hard to stay out of World War II, could fight so savagely once it entered. How could American men descend on Normandy like "deadly hordes of predators"? Why are some groups so good at fighting, and some so poor?

In his *The Soul of Battle,* Hanson demonstrated that no army has fought well when its objective was to enslave or conquer people. But armies out to save its people or to liberate others—think of Patton's race to the Rhine or Sherman's rampage through Georgia—fought with astonishing passion, and won.

> *"Any activity that gives us a sense of purpose and accomplishment, that makes us feel glad to be alive, can help us care for and feed our brain," writes Dr. John J. Ratey, a Harvard Medical School professor of psychiatry, in* A User's Guide to the Brain. *"Passion heals."*

Passion, inflamed by belief and purpose, wins. Passion can be found in the soul of battle and the heart of a great business. Experts in psychology even contend that passion is therapeutic. "It heals," one has written.

Belief and passion: Is this any way to run a company? Give me process, a Gant chart, a system, the hardened executive insists. Give me something concrete: Seven steps. Eight keys.

We try. But when we search for the hard nuggets

that drive success, we don't find hard nuggets. We find something softer. We find that the equation for success seems elusive, defying all intelligent efforts to reduce it to action steps.

Success, it seems, comes from that mysterious place called our souls.

Several years ago, representatives of seven famous investment banking firms flew into Seattle, Washington, to pitch Starbucks. Each firm made its pitch and impressed the audience so much that CEO Howard Schultz later reported that he couldn't tell the seven firms apart—except for one tiny thing.

"Commitment and passion. That was the difference," Schultz told *Fortune* magazine in 1997.

That's it? Passion? Not skill, acumen, talent, experience—*passion?*

If passion is the answer, what can a business-person do?

Can you "action item" belief and passion?

Can you write "Instill passion" in a business plan? Not without risking your job.

Could you write "Recruit optimists" into your human resources plan? Only at the same risk. And then what do you do—screen for employees who say they loved *Pygmalion* and identified with *Rocky*?

You could struggle for a lifetime to translate these intangibles into your plan.

> *"No sense being pessimistic. Wouldn't work anyway."*
> —*Bumper sticker*

That's why so few companies soar. If every business could reduce belief and passion into easy steps, almost every business would have.

What should managers do? Build something that

fills you with passion, and then spread its flames into every corner of your business.

Listen to Pearce, Pottruck, Hanson, and Landes: Belief and passion grow businesses. Clients love passionate people and passionate businesses because passion stimulates them—they feel it and feel better, too—and because they know that passion produces great work.

Triumph, then, belongs to those who believe. Belief steels us with the courage to take the risks that the faithless avoid, and to reap the rewards that follow— to realize that our lives grow in proportion to our courage.

So the next time two paths appear before you, avoid the one of least resistance; a path with no obstacles rarely leads anywhere. Take instead the path that runs along the cliff—that one, the one without any guardrails.

Take that path, and know that the exhilaration of the ride and the pride you feel when you reach the end will inspire you to take that path again and again.

And that experience, one day, will make you more money. But that experience, every day, will make you more fulfilled, more complete and more alive.

—Harry Beckwith, October 1, 2002

Appendix

Checklist: Questions to Ask in Building an Exceptional Business

FIRST PRINCIPLE

What really matters to us?
Where do we want to be in five years?

> Why? Are we sure?
> How do we want our lives, at work and outside it, to be different?
> What key changes must we make to get there from here?

Never mind what we have done or others have done: What is possible?
What would clients think was remarkable?
If we were starting from scratch today, what would we do differently?

> How would we organize ourselves to better serve clients?
> What would we add?
> What would we eliminate?

How should we start to make these changes, beginning today?

If we were competing against us, where would we attack us?

How do we shore up that weakness?

ADDING DEEPER INSIGHT

Which ten or twelve clients, friends, industry insiders, or other individuals can give us the most insight about improving our business?

GETTING TO THE WHITE HOT CENTER

Who makes up the White Hot Center of our industry?
Which members do we have contact with? Which do we not?
What should we do to increase our influence with these people?

GETTING THE KEY CLIENTS

What three to four prospective and acquirable clients would have the most long-term impact on our business—as uniquely strong references?
How can we begin to convert them into clients?

ATTACKING OUR INDUSTRY'S WEAKNESS

What is the greatest flaw in our industry, in the perception of prospects and clients?

How can we dramatically eliminate this flaw?

What stereotype do outsiders have of people in our business?

How can we overcome this?

OUR BRAND

Is our brand unique?
Is it vivid?
Is it simple?
Does it communicate a clear and powerful message, in the way we most want and need to communicate?
Is it inviting?

OUR NAME

Is our name distinctive?
Is it memorable?
Is it brief enough to be processed and remembered?
Does it express or imply an important message?
Does the value and equity of our current name outweigh the value of changing it to a more powerful and useful name?

Can it be pronounced easily, even musically?

Will most people have to ask how to spell it? If so, can you easily explain how to spell it?

Is it short? (Eleven letters and four syllables should be the maximum.)

Does it have the traits to make it memorable—is it unique, sensory, and outstanding?

Is it interesting? Does it have "story value"?

Is it authentic? Is it who we really are?

Can our employees say the name proudly?

Does it set the right tone?

Is it different enough from competitors' names?

Is it acceptable to virtually every important prospect?

Does it make some people uneasy? (The answer "yes" is desirable.)

Does it express or imply a desirable message?

Is it rich with meaning? Does it imply more than one positive message? (Some good names do not meet this test, but many great names do.)

OUR PRICE

What does our price communicate about the value of our work?

Is our pricing absolutely clear?

Is it so simple a prospect understands it immediately? And so simple that it does not delay or distract the client?

OUR PACKAGE: THE VISUAL AUDIT

Look at every point where our prospects come into contact with us—from business cards and signage to attire and envelopes:

Does each contact make a strong impression?

Does each say, "This firm is special"?

Does each contact clearly convey a sense of quality and professionalism?

Are the messages at each point consistent with each other?

OUR COMMUNICATIONS

Are our messages brief and to the point?

Does every word count—or are there unnecessary and wasted words?

Do we immediately convey our point of difference?

Do we clearly and convincingly communicate the distinctive benefit of working with us?

Do we provide strong proof for each of our claims?

If the person never reads a word of the message, does the communication still convey a sense of quality?

Does the reader feel engaged by the copy? Does it speak to him and his wants and needs—or do we talk too much about ourselves?

OUR PRESENTATIONS

Do our images, by themselves, convey an unmistakable sense of quality and professionalism?

Is each slide necessary? Does each one deliver its message better than words alone can?

Are slides kept to a minimum, so that our audience will focus on our people rather than our slides?

Does each image convey no more than three succinct points?

Can any point be made in half as many words?

Are the images interesting yet appropriate?

Are the words engaging and interesting?

Is our presentation about the client and his needs— or is it about us?

Is the presentation compelling without being immodest?

Is our presentation human, warm, inviting, and personal? Are there moments where it is too institutional?

Are our testimonials powerful and believable?

Do we use stories to make our message clearer and more interesting?

OUR SERVICE

Are 20 percent of our clients thrilled with us?

Are all but 10 percent of our clients very pleased with us, and what we do for them?

What plans do we have for graciously eliminating that 10 percent?

Is our receptionist warm, welcoming, and optimistic?

If not, what must we do—this week—to fix that?

Does someone feel extraordinarily welcome when they enter our doors?

Are phone calls answered and forwarded in near real time?

What can we do to ensure that they are?

Do we return calls or follow up on contacts in near real time?

Do we follow up every contact with a prospect or client within twenty-four hours?

Do we have a regular and closely followed program for thanking clients and prospects at least once a year?

Are we doing something special for our loyal clients at least once a year?

Do each of our special clients clearly know they are special to us?

When we make a promise to a client, do we make sure to put it in writing so we will know what we have promised and what to do—and they will know exactly what to expect from us, and when?

A READING LIST FOR GROWING A BUSINESS

General

The *New York Times,* particularly "Science Times" (published each Tuesday). A remarkable newspaper, business, and institution. The "Science Times" section stands out for translating important discoveries in the natural and social sciences—including psychology and customer behavior—into clear and even engaging prose. A model of good communicating—well written and well edited—the *Times* stands alone.

The New Yorker. This magazine has made a surprising yet subtle transformation from being an arbiter of taste and style for decades to a barometer of both today. Deft at isolating changes in popular culture and the arts that reflect broader cultural changes, valuable for providing a forum for Malcolm Gladwell's probes into psychological research and for outstanding writing, and—thanks to the world's best cartoons—skilled at making us laugh while we think—and despite these changes, a second-to-none source of insight into the lives and values of America's "educated affluent."

Marketing

The Marketing Imagination, Theodore Levitt. Excellent big-picture view.

Positioning: The Battle for Your Mind, Al Ries and Jack Trout. A model of clarity, this classic manages to be both fun and helpful in focusing on where marketing begins.

Overload

The Attention Economy, Thomas Davenport and John Beck. A detailed case for the overabundance of information in the world today, a description of its effects, and some strategies for dealing with the consequences to your company.

Trust

Bowling Alone: The Collapse and Revival of American Community, Robert Putnam. Not all agree with his conclusions, but his insights on the decline of trust seem irrefutable.

Trust: The Social Virtues and the Creation of Prosperity, Francis Fukuyama. Heavy reading at times, but sound and inspiring.

Cultural Changes and Trends

Utne Reader, monthly magazine. Covers the fringes and the innovators, the people who change first.

Visits to bellwether cities: Seattle and Portland. The defiant individualism of this region—most obvious in its residents' resistance to other people's fads and fashions—results in two cities filled with mavericks and pioneers. Fusion jazz, Nirvana, Starbucks, Nordstrom, Nintendo, Gus Van Sant, Jimi Hendrix—all started here. Portland's *Willamette Week* newspaper offers early peeks into what's next in American culture.

Clear Communicating

The Elements of Style, William Strunk and E. B. White. Never equaled, probably because no one has been able to summon the courage to write a book that might be compared with this classic. Useful on concreteness, brevity, preciseness, and "visual" words.

On Writing Well, William Zinsser. A perfect model of what it preaches: writing you understand the instant you read it.

Cat's Cradle, Kurt Vonnegut, Jr. Irreverent, literally—a spoof of religion—and perhaps the clearest book ever written—as well as among the most engaging.

Storytelling

Cat's Cradle, Kurt Vonnegut, Jr. See above. Watch how the author does it—how, among other things, he intrigues readers about what comes next—a key to storytelling that engages and keeps a reader and audience.

The Psychology of Clients

Influence: The Psychology of Persuasion, Robert B. Cialdini. Useful, accessible, and popular.

Motivation and Personality, Abraham Maslow. A beginning point to understanding buyers' behavior. No psychologist has equaled Maslow's impact on marketing.

The Soul of a New Machine, Tracy Kidder. A well-told story that will deepen your understanding of how techies think, live, and work.

Journal of Personality and Social Psychology. Ponderous except to psychologists—and perhaps even to them—this journal is a leading source of information on human behavior, including buying behavior.

Psychology Today. Certainly not scientifically rigorous but not scientifically irresponsible either, this publication translates psychology for the masses and can point you to other sources to deepen your understanding on a topic.

Worthy Works of Fiction That Explore Human Character

Anna Karenina, Leo Tolstoy. Dazzling and perceptive.

The Portrait of a Lady, Henry James. A brilliant examination of the lives and traits of the wealthy.

The Great Gatsby, F. Scott Fitzgerald. Timeless, particularly on upward mobility, ambition, acquisitiveness—all this and the most lyrical final three paragraphs ever written.

The Catcher in the Rye, J. D. Salinger. A map to young people's brains—their disenchantment, angst over the opposite sex, and confusion.

Branding and Design

@issue. Sponsored by Potlach Corporation and guided by editor Peter Lawrence, this thoughtful, accessible, and well-designed publication explains America's best corporate design.

One magazine. Handsome exploration of the world's best design, with a strong philosophy that form follows function and that design works as beautifully as it looks.

Building a Dream: The Art of Disney Architecture, Beth Dunlop. A behind-the-facades look at Disney architecture—from theme parks to hotels to corporate headquarters—and a reminder of the influence of packaging, environment, and detail.

Communication Arts Design Annual. Even the strategically dubious work—and it abounds in these attractive glossy pages—demonstrates the infinite options in design.

Niketown stores, numerous locations. Outstanding example of space that reinforces a brand and creates an inviting and memorable experience.

Other examples:
    Nike headquarters building, Beaverton, Oregon.
    Wieden + Kennedy advertising agency headquarters, Powell's Bookstore (downtown site), and Portland International Airport, Portland, Oregon.
    Camden Yards baseball park, Baltimore, Maryland.
    The Grand Bar (SoHo) and Tribeca Grand Hotel, New York City.
    Asia de Cuba restaurants, New York City.
    The East Bay Club, Chicago, Illinois.
    Ed Debevic's restaurant (faithful execution of a brand), Chicago, Illinois (other Lettuce Entertain

You restaurants in Chicago also are worth viewing).

ESPN restaurant and bar, Orlando, Florida (excellent example of extending and supporting a company brand, in creating a distinctive property in a crowded market—sports bars—and providing an excellent customer experience).

Wild Rumpus bookstore, Minneapolis.

Hotel Monaco, San Francisco and Seattle.

Chiat\Day advertising headquarters building, Venice, California.

Microsoft Museum, Bellevue, Washington.

Gaslamp Quarter, San Diego, California.

Target stores (excellent example of visual clarity), nationwide.

Kohl's stores (excellent example of speed and convenience), nationwide.

Felix restaurant, Peninsula Hotel, Hong Kong. Unforgettable.

Restoration Hardware stores, nationwide.

Sephora store, Paris, France, Champs-Elysées site.

Worthy Works of Nonfiction, Notable for Their Clarity, Power of Expression, and Understanding of Human Nature

Slouching Towards Bethlehem and *The White Album,* Joan Didion. The first book includes Didion's brilliant essay "Some Dreamers of the Golden Dream" and both books capture the soul and spirit of the baby boom generation thirty years ago, a spirit that still informs them today.

Oranges, John McPhee. Beautifully demonstrates that everything is interesting if you look deeply—a lesson for anyone planning to advertise or publicize a business: If you dig, the stories are always there.

The Headmaster, John McPhee. Also interesting as a character study of an educator, leader, and a person driven by a passion, in the person of Frank Boyden, the former headmaster of Deerfield Academy, and the dramatic result—the turnaround of a service business, Boyden's school.

Working, Studs Terkel. A peek into Americans of all types, in their own words, stressing their work's role in their lives. Also a useful reference and reminder of different American idioms.

The Double Helix, James Watson. Perhaps the rarest of page turners, a spellbinder about science—in this case the early 1950s race of several scientists to unlock the mysteries of the human gene and, with it, win an almost certain Nobel Prize. Another excellent insight into the thinking of scientists.

An Interview with Harry Beckwith

What prompted this third book?

There was so much more to say. Many of the ideas were inspired by audience members at my speeches. When I realized my books had not answered those questions, I started writing. The section in this book on cold calling, for example, was prompted by an audience question at Liberty Property Trust's national meeting in 1997.

What surprised you most about the first two books?
Learning that the most popular entry in *Selling the Invisible* was the story about Meryl Streep. Frankly, when I signed off on the manuscript, that section was the one I wished I had left out.

Why?
It seemed too fluffy. Its message was right; it *does* help to think of life as resembling high school but not college. But I worried that the story would undermine the seriousness of my intent in writing the book.

This story suggests one tenet of marketing: *You never know.* People—the core of marketing—defy prediction.

What has been most gratifying about your books?
The opportunities to learn more, by exploring companies all over the world. You learn from speaking and consulting every day—on a good day, every few minutes.

Second, the travel. I would never have seen Warsaw without these books, and neither my son Will nor I ever will forget our trip to Switzerland and Paris, sponsored by my generous clients at Hewlett-Packard Europe.

And of course, the royalties are nice, particularly with four children.

You repeatedly cast doubt on the Internet and the New Economy. Do you feel vindicated by the recent events, such as the "Fall of the Dot.coms"?

The noble answer is no, but my answer is yes—although maybe I got lucky. My thinking about the Internet was based on my experiences. I was an early adopter and heavy user; when Internet users used to be allotted a hundred hours a month before incurring extra charges, I always ran out by the last week. But I paid for and purchased *nothing*. No books, no auctions, nothing—except a laughably cheap e-subscription to the electronic edition of the *Wall Street Journal*.

There were many reasons to suspect that the Internet would not revolutionize our lives. Most people hate gadgets, for one. People who do like gizmos often cannot figure them out; men's VCRs blink "12:00" all day long, too. The Internet also takes time, and we don't have much. Should we believe that people will turn off *Friends* and *Survivor* to chat with strangers electronically—especially when *Friends* is free, on a huge screen, and the Friends are beautiful and say much wittier things than you ever find in a chat room?

And one more consideration. Whatever business the Internet might grab, the temporary losers will fight back. If the Internet sells content, traditional content companies will retaliate. And they will do it with established brands—which are *huge* weapons. Will people read an online-only business publication, for example, once the *Wall Street Journal* launches wsj.com? Which content will readers prefer? The content they have come to trust—the brand they have come to trust.

My growing conviction about the power of brands suggests only a few Internet-only businesses will survive. Amazon has a chance—especially if it merges with a longer-established brand—but it's worth noting that Amazon itself is not a formidable brand. Millions of people know it, but few feel loyalty to it.

Who will succeed on the Internet?

As eBay's fast start suggests, auctions are probably a killer app for the Internet—although the prices people are receiving at these auctions and quality-control issues could kill it. People who thought they could make a killing by finding a very desperate bidder somewhere in the world often sell at a loss online—an amazing phenomenon.

And sex is the great American pastime—as perhaps suggested by the fact that next to Mark McGwire's and Sammy Sosa's shattering of Babe Ruth's seventy-year-old home run record, the biggest news in baseball in the past twenty years was a couple having sex in a hotel room in Toronto's SkyDome, in full view of the appreciative fans. Pornography isn't regarded as a large industry because business publications—for obvious reasons—ignore it. Yet pornography takes in more revenue—at least $10 billion annually at incredibly high margins—than the NFL, NBA, and Major League Baseball *combined*. Pornography is a mammoth industry.

So do you believe there is a New Economy?

Not an economy as revolutionary as the word "new" suggests. As Michael Porter has said, genuinely disruptive technologies are rare—and the New Economy is predicated heavily on them. Even if you create a disruptive technology, there is no assurance people will want, buy, and use it. People are conservative; most dislike disruption.

The hoopla over the New Economy reminds me of the experience marketers had for years when they ventured into technology-based companies, particularly medical device companies. In those companies, development and product refinement is everything. Marketing is subordinate. You must tell the world that your gizmo has better doodads than Brand Y's. The idea of customer benefit is secondary in these companies; they assume that people want and buy technological modifications because they represent forward steps—something faster or smaller, for example. But who really cares? When the New Economy din was loudest, it sounded like that—like the Innovators and Techies describing a life in which everyone felt like them and loved what they loved. It wasn't unlike opera fans taking over the popular conversation and insisting that opera was about to change everything.

My Favorite Part: Acknowledgments

Most authors write their acknowledgments during that moment of relief when their book is finally done. But I do not feel relieved; I feel sad. This book has kept me months of good company. It has awakened me suddenly and willed me to sleep, from its awkward first months to this moment when it must enter the world. Like watching my children, I hate seeing this book leave; it is my favorite. All of me is in here.

I also feel thankful. I wrote this with a hundred helpers, including some who are gone—several teachers and my beloved Clive Davies, for example— and others who are far away and connected with me only by memories. In thanking these people who blessed me, I remember Picasso, justifying his large fee for a sketch that he'd drawn in minutes. The sketch didn't take minutes, he insisted; it took him his whole life.

So thanks to the following people, for debts that cover a lifetime.

Cliff Greene and Sue Crolick, for starting all this.

Eric Vrooman, for your lasting influence; Steve Kaplan, for your suggestion a decade ago that changed everything; Jay Novak, for letting me practice on your readers; and Lynette Lamb, for buffing, polishing, and rebuilding.

My great teachers: Harriet Evenson, James Robinson, Des Kahrs, Clifford Rowe, Kurt Vonnegut, Jr.,

E. B. White, William Zinsser, John McPhee, John Till-man, and Stanford professors David Potter, Ron Reb-holz, David Kennedy, Robert Horn, Paul Robinson, and William Clebsch.

The people of Warner Books, who demonstrate that Southern hospitality stretches to midtown New York: Rick Wolff, Dan Ambrosio, Mel Parker, Sharon Krassney, Jimmy Franco, Jean Griffin, Andrew Fleish-man, Chris Dao, and two talented women who keep making me look better, Giorgetta Bell McRee and Bernadette Evangelist.

The clients of a lifetime: Stephanie Prem and Peter Glanville of Wells Fargo and Lowry Hill.

Ty Votaw and the many special women and men of the Ladies' Professional Golf Association; Stan Barkey of State Farm Insurance, another wonderfully welcoming company; Larry Stratton of Service Master; John Coban of Lasalle Bonds; Jim Getz and the many Donahues of Federated Investors, who not only so-licited my thoughts but applied them; Jamie DePeau of Merck-Medco; and John Tillotson of ventures far and wide.

More thanks, too, to Mark Stevens of Northern Trust; the unforgettable Susan Tinsley of Ivey Mechanical; venture capitalist Pete Thomas; the nonpareil Said Hilal of Applied Medical; Roger McGuin of The Byrds, for your insights that helped me understand creativity; Bruce Ozda of EDS; Rick Salzer, wherever you are; F. Lee Bailey, for stories and good companionship, even while we shared opposing views; Christer Hane-falk of Logographia, Stockholm; the very nice women and Fools of Motley Fool.

No less, thanks to Mark Hughes of Bell South, Roxanna Frost of Microsoft, a host of men and women with Hewlett-Packard Europe; former U.S. Postmaster General Bill Henderson; John Schultz; Malcolm Gladwell, for thoughts that changed the way I think, my highest compliment; John Wotring and the special people of Primrose.

A beyond-words thanks to J.

Over a dozen writers and editors from the *Wall Street Journal, The New Yorker,* and the *New York Times,* who provided leads, insight, and inspiration.

The many people of Stanford University in the 1970s, particularly the generous ones in Admissions—or perhaps they assumed my 2.26 high school GPA was someone's typo. Whatever their reasons, they changed my life.

Joyce Agnew, Katie Barrett, Claire Canavan, Jane Delson, Dean Fouquette, Steve Gould, Mark Hughes, Greg Kunz, Cathy Madison, Jeanine Mayfield, Bob O'Connor, Leftheris and Jane Papageorgiou, Cathy Wornstaff Phillips, Jeannie Pierri, Mary Beth Powers, Becky Robertson, Sandra Simmons, Mitzi Stepp, Cindy Weber, and Robert Wilson.

Barb and John and Joel and Judy. I hope to thank you again in other ways.

Some unique sources of insight: you gracious people who allowed me to peek behind the curtains of your companies; Roy Martin of Dialog; plus a special thanks to the people of Northern Trust and State Farm Insurance, and Rita Schaefer and Paul Coglin of Houghton Mifflin/McDougal Littel, for your generous advice.

Janice Eaves, an angel on Drew Avenue.

Becky Powell, David Macy-Beckwith, and Valerie Fouquette, for your patience, laughter, and love.

Clive Davies, a hero. You run with the angels, dear friend. You always did.

Harry IV, Will, Cole, and Cooper, four more miracles. I carry you everywhere.

Alice, especially for your faith.

And finally, my dad. Part legend and part father, he cast a long shadow. His steps were long, too, but blazed a good trail. I followed some of those steps, lost others, and—realizing that even giants stumble now and then—plotted some of my own. No one achieves perfection, but Harry Beckwith, Jr., walked right to the edge and peeked in, and perfection smiled back.

You were, Dad, and always will be, a gift.

—*Harry Beckwith*

**BUSINESS
PLUS**

Recognized as one of the world's most prestigious business imprints, Business Plus specializes in publishing books that are on the cutting edge. Like you, to be successful we always strive to be ahead of the curve.

Business Plus titles encompass a wide range of books and interests—including important business management works, state-of-the-art personal financial advice, noteworthy narrative accounts, the latest in sales and marketing advice, individualized career guidance, and autobiographies of the key business leaders of our time.

Our philosophy is that business is truly global in every way, and that today's business reader is looking for books that are both entertaining and educational. To find out more about what we're publishing, please check out the Business Plus blog at:

www.businessplusblog.com